American Corn

seed time:
True Short Stories in the Life of a Child of the Greatest Generation

By T.S. Malinowski

Tate Publishing, LLC

American Corn by T.S. Malinowski

Copyright © 2005 by T.S. Malinowski. All rights reserved.

Published in the United States of America
by Tate Publishing, LLC
127 East Trade Center Terrace
Mustang, OK 73064
(888) 361–9473

Book design copyright © 2005 by Tate Publishing, LLC. All rights reserved.

No part of this publication may be reproduced, stored in a retrieval system or transmitted in any way by any means, electronic, mechanical, photocopy, recording or otherwise without the prior permission of the author except as provided by USA copyright law.

ISBN: 1-59886-14-8-4

Table Of Contents

Introduction 7

Love, Patience, Persistence and Endurance 11
Something Old, Something New 17
Joy In The Small Things 23
Grandma's House 29
What A Difference a Bike Makes 37
Sisterly Love 39
Church Boy 47
The Dogs Of My Youth 51
The Principle Of Ice Cream 59
Enjoy Where You Are 63
Life In The Hallway 69
Any Ball Game Will Do 73
The Kite and the Snake 77
Monopoly By Storm 81
The Black Box In My Room 87
Oh! To Read 93
My Fishing Father 99
Track Is The Ticket 105
Life Changing Coach 113
Finding The One 123
The Gifts From Others 129
Dad Under Fire 133

Foreword

Everyone knows the 1950's and 60's were a unique time in history. Growing up with the birth of the television, the Cold War in full swing, and before the invention of the microprocessor meant what is now so loosely termed 'the simple life' really was exactly that—simple. What you are about to read will give you an intimate glimpse at a young boy growing up in Western New York. A time in history where the principles and childhood values taught to him by his parents laid the foundation for his entire life. Not only have these principles impacted the lives of his children and grandchildren, but also the lives of thousands of young men and women whom Ted has taught in the public school system over the last three decades.

I have known Ted for over thirty years. He is one of the most principled men I have ever met. Having read his stories, I now understand a little more of what helped to mold and shape this young mind into what he has become to so many people today. He is a trusted friend, mentor and confidant. I am not surprised at all by the clarity with which Ted takes you back to the events of his youth. Over the years I have heard bits and pieces of his boyhood experiences and antics myself. From cover to cover, I am reminded of the movie "A Christmas Story" where the young lad longs for the Holy Grail of Christmas gifts–the Red Ryder 200 shot range model air rifle. That would have been Ted.

This keyhole view into the life of a boy raised on American family values, rooted in a strong Polish heritage, will cause you to laugh, think and cry. If you are a baby boomer it will help transcend you to yesteryear. Those were the days of *The Lone Ranger, Dennis the Menace*, and *My Three Sons*. That was a time when right was right and wrong was wrong. There was no middle ground or concern over being 'politically correct.' You spoke your mind. A time when true heroes were honorable, embodied integrity and were role models for future generations. You wanted to be like them.

If you are the offspring of a baby boomer, these refreshing snapshots in time will give you a peek into what your parents may have experienced in their youth. Here you will have a chance to pause and consider what life could be like for you and your family. You only need to take the time to make lasting memories along the way.

For as long as I can remember Ted has been a teacher and has taught me a lot about life. What he passes along to us through these short stories will help us all to remember that life is precious if we live in the moment. I hope that you will enjoy these very personal childhood memories from my good friend as much as I have.

Randy Vetter

Introduction

In 1995 I had decided to leave a teaching position I had held for twenty-three years. That one decision set into motion an entire chain of events. That is how all decisions are, as Dad and Mom had taught me.

Janice, my wife of twenty-nine years, thought that we wanted to live in the south. As providence would have it, the principal of a high school in South Carolina called. He had been conducting a national search for an experienced industrial technology teacher. After looking at my professional credentials and a background check, he had already concluded that I was his man, before he had even made the call. Janice and I were both astounded at this event.

I moved to the south and started work. As time went on I began to slip into a state of deep depression. The principal was a superb person to work for, and the school system was exceptional. I missed my wife, who is my best friend, my children, Wade and Tawnya, and some life-long friends. Janice stayed up north for three and a half months, trying very hard to sell our home. We have a nice home, but it never was sold. Thank God!

I was doing an excellent job of beating myself up, while our finances and business were falling apart. I was at the very lowest part of my life. It was at this point that I began to write some true short stories about my childhood. The writing and the thought process caused me to arrest my emotional descent. I began to realize how influential and supportive Dad and Mom were, along with friends and family. I actually began to feel the joy I had felt as a child through these writings.

I suddenly started to realize how often providence would put just the right person in my life at just the correct moment, to put me back on the right path. I noticed that many of these people were part of the "Greatest Generation," as it has become known. Dad and Mom were part of that generation. They were great teachers of life's principles, without my knowing they were teaching. Their teaching was in the form of the life they lived. It has often seemed that these types of people have surrounded me. I did not know it at the time, of course, but it certainly became clear as I examined my life. I have concluded that none of this was a coincidence. I am so thankful that most of the time I had made the choice to listen to these great teachers.

I now know that all of us have people who come into our lives with a promise, but are we willing to listen? I hope that as you read these true, short stories you will be reminded of your own joys growing up and the warmth of caring people, who, like angels, have stepped down from heaven for just a moment with their message, to make your life better for you and those you come in contact with.

Then, you too, will become the seed planted

and nurtured by this country's "Greatest Generation." Their lessons are planted deep within us, and it is now our responsibility to plant for the next growth. Enjoy!

Love, Patience, Persistence and Endurance

*I*t was a very sunny spring morning. The sunlight was streaming through the bedroom window, followed by a gorgeous breeze. The spring air always smells so sweet and clean and makes you want to get up out of your bed and not miss a moment of the day.

I got up from my bed and proceeded to walk to the bathroom in my loose hanging, Davey Crockett pajamas. I could hear the washing machine running as I approached the bathroom, where it was located. Mom always pulled the machine over to the edge of the bathtub when she was using it. The machine was always a curious device as it vibrated and danced through its operations. It was a real attraction on this beautiful morning. I approached the machine with great curiosity. I could see that the agitator was twisting the clothes back and forth. Next to it was a spin-dry device which spun the clothes very fast to remove most of the water. Then Mom would take them out and hang them on a clothesline. This was my first close-up look at all of this machinery in action.

The wringer device produced the most attention-getting feat. The two, hard-rubber rollers were always rolling when the machine was running. Their job was to squeeze the water out of the clothes when you ran the clothes in between them. The rollers exerted a great amount of pressure against each other. Their white surfaces glistened in the sunlight as they turned. The soapy water produced the colors of the rainbow against their pure white surfaces. How could such a beautiful device be so harmful? I decided that it was not harmful because I had seen Felix the cat on the Saturday cartoons go through the rollers, and after coming out flattened, he blew on his thumb and inflated himself once again.

What could there be to fear? I decided to run my fingers across the bottom white roller as it squeezed the pretty shades of pink and blue soapy water out over the perfectly white roller. I touched it very softly at first and then I ran my four fingers back and forth through the soapy sheet of water. My Davey Crockett pajama sleeves were now getting very wet and beginning to sag under the weight of the soaking water.

It was just a little part of the right sleeve that got caught between the two pure white rollers. The machine seemed to grab just that little piece of water-soaked fabric. It was as if it had teeth. The pure white rollers began to pull the pajamas in between the two rollers. I was now watching as the water was being squeezed from my pajamas. I pulled my hand back into the sleeve and up to the shoulder of the shirt. I knew that the cartoon cat was just a cartoon and this was real life. In fact it was my life. The pain was just too much for a little boy of four not to scream as the white wringers finally got to my fingers and pulled them in as if it was a starved creature.

Mom heard that terrible and hopeless scream as she hung the clothes out on the line to dry. She knew with that motherly intuition what was causing the scream as she ran for the bathroom. Once she was in the room, she did not say a word. She just went straight to work and hit the release lever, which released all pressure from the rollers. The rollers had already reached my elbow and had begun to roll up the flesh along with the pajama sleeve. It's a good thing a four-year-old's arm is so small, or more damage would have been done. I collapsed in Mom's arms as the rollers released their grip on my right arm, and then I blacked out. The next time I opened my eyes I realized my head was in my Mom's lap. We were in Dad's car driving to the doctor's office as a fast as he could go. I did not know how Dad got home so fast, in order to pick us up, but he did.

The next thing I remember is waking up on a cold, black table with a big, bright light up above me. The doctor was talking and putting some kind of green salve on my right arm. He was telling my parents that the chance of my ever straightening that arm again was extremely slim. My Mom said, "He will!"

The next time I awoke I was at home with my right arm in a sling, and it was all bandaged up. Mom began explaining how we were going to work together on this project. I really did not know how serious the injury was. I was not worried, and, of course, I believed Mom. God gives us wonderful gifts in our youth. The particular one I'm thinking of is how flexible we are to adversity in our youth. Mom didn't ever say that I had a severe injury, or that the recovery wouldn't be complete. I just figured that everything would be all right.

Mom, as good mothers do, went right to work. She started saving the cardboard six-pack cartons that Pepsi bottles came in. Cans were not available then. My arm would be in a sling for about six weeks, so Mom had time to prepare for her own rehab program. The doctor said that the bone was not broken, but the tendons and muscles were probably damaged. He thought the arm could not be completely straightened.

Mom's goal was to straighten and strengthen that right arm! Let the games begin!

The next six weeks seemed to fly by that spring, and Mom was ready. She was standing by the kitchen sink pointing to the small, shiny, red tricycle when she said, "Take these empty six-pack cartons and load two at a time on the back of your tricycle. Then take them to the front door. Unload them there and come back and get two more." Once I had all ten at the front door, she instructed me to reload them and take them back to the kitchen door. She made sure that I did all of this with my right arm, of course. We would do this routine two to four times a day. The first time it was very painful just to lift that empty carton. When Mom saw that it was no longer hurting, she put an empty bottle in each six-pack. It would hurt again and she just said, "Good." It wasn't long before I had six empty bottles in each carton. I felt I was making progress because the arm was becoming straighter. That's when Mom began to fill the first bottle in the pack with water, and the pain started again. In a few weeks all of the bottles were full, and the arm was completely straight. Mom's goal was to build up the muscles of the arm and have it be as straight as my left arm. Her goal was accomplished. She has continued, to this day, to tell me I could do anything I set my mind to do.

It was years before I knew what had been done to me physically and mentally. I participated in wrestling, baseball, football, basketball, and track, never even realizing that my Mom saw me doing all these things and more in her mind many years before.

Something Old, Something New

   *T*imes seemed to be much simpler in the early 50's, except for the atomic bomb. I was thrilled to listen to the Lone Ranger on the radio, and then it happened. I went to Grandma's, where my Aunts and Uncles were all visiting. There it was, the first television in our family. This was the first one I had ever laid eyes on. It appeared to be just a wooden box with an eight-inch window that you could not see into. We all had to wait until dark to see what this window would show us. It was not that it had to be dark; it's just that the programs did not start until six o'clock in the evening. I didn't know that was the real reason. I can just tell you that I did not want to wait.

  To occupy my time until the magic moment, I went outside on that very warm August night and caught some fireflies in a jar. I came back into the house and set the glowing jar on the table next to the wonder-box. What a sight it was to behold when Aunt Aggie turned on that wonder-box called a television! I really wondered if it would work, because it took a long time to warm up. You could count on the fireflies to blink on time. It was quite a sight in that room that night. Grandma, aunts, uncles, Mom, Dad, and my sister, all of us basking in the blue light of that television and the yellow-green light of the dependable fireflies. The fireflies were always more reliable and more fun than the television, as far as I was concerned.

It is remarkable how that television brought the entire family together for the evening. The gathering was always on Sundays. The dinner table would be whirling with conversation on what might be viewed that evening. What a change from the radio. The imagination is a personal and powerful thing, which was stimulated constantly by the radio. Now you did not have to use your imagination. The screen gave you the image, not your brain.

One evening we were all at home when Dad came home from work with a big box. My sister and I closed in on the box immediately, because Dad never came home with surprises like this. He and Mom opened the box, and there it was, our very own television set. Our family life changed that very moment. Now, the entire family did not have to get together for that Sunday meal at Grandma's. All of the discussions and joy around what seemed to be an aircraft carrier sized dining room table would be missed. We could now watch television from the comfort of our own little home.

Saturdays became much different. We could start the morning off with a good dose of the Lone Ranger, followed by Wild Bill Hickcock and Roy Rogers. Then we would get more current shows, like Sky King and Captain Midnight. Sometimes there would be a space show called Flash Gordon. This gave us fuel for our imaginations, because in the afternoons we went outside and played those characters out. Very often we made up our own stories and adventures. The fight was always for the good, and it was understood that the good guys always won. Sometimes you had to be the bad guy, because it was your turn. It was not so bad, because once your character was killed off, you could be the good guy again. It sure made you recognize who was who.

The toy weapon of choice was the Fanner Fifty. It was a six-shooter revolver that came with real leather holsters. It looked just like the one the Lone Ranger used. We all knew that real guns were extremely dangerous. Bobby's father was a hunter. We had no interest in messing with the real thing. Eliminating the bad guy and standing up for what was right and good in God's eyes was the goal. Protecting the good seemed to be what dominated our play. It all seemed so clear. As we all watched our favorite TV programs, we were influenced by characters that had very high standards. No one was ever killed in these programs. They were always wounded in the arm or leg. It was always assumed that the courts were sending them to jail for their bad deeds. We would kill the character off in our playing, because we could not go through the court stuff. If the bad guy had still been around, we would not have been able to keep playing.

Sometimes we would get together with some of our model planes. After we had assembled them, we would hold them in our hands and pretend we were flying them. We would then have these dogfights and be yelling at each other as if we were on the radios of the aircraft. It was always very exciting to be a pilot.

One day I was flying my plane through my Dad's garden, all around the stalks of corn. It was a gorgeous, sunny day, and there were no clouds in the sky. For some unexplainable reason, I looked up in the sky and saw a flash, and then just a wisp of smoke. I wondered what it was. That evening my Dad came home from work and told us that a B-47 had exploded and then parts of it had fallen to the ground in the little town of North Collins. The evening news came on the TV and told of the crash. Dad said, "Lets go see if we can see it." We drove there, and sure enough, we saw a piece of wing and some other metal pieces on the ground. No metal struck anyone on the ground. I think the crew of two got out. This was a topic of discussion with my friends and me, because now flying could have other events besides being shot down. We later found out that the plane suffered from what was called metal fatigue. We had to find out what that was, so we all were doing research to learn about it. This caused us to use the encyclopedia that Mom had purchased. A research frenzy, which any good teacher would have been delighted with, happened that summer. We found out that metal would actually become tired and break after repeated bending. This resulted in wing failure. It also caused my friends and me to admire Air Force pilots even more than we already did.

The TV and events around us caused us to

be curious. The need to learn by looking into other sources of information, like the encyclopedia, became exciting research for all of us. We would learn more about other related areas, and then it all became like a big adventure. Mom encouraged us to be curious. She loved to listen to our findings.

Joy in the Small Things

We definitely were not a financially rich family. Yet, it was realized by all of us that we had more than enough of all we ever really needed. The season of Christmas just seemed to magnify everything that is good in the life of this seven-year-old boy.

The small, cement block home we lived in had a fireplace and gas furnace right there in the living room. The windows were of the single pane, uninsulated variety, which doesn't exist today. A most remarkable thing would happen upon these glass panes when it became very cold outside. It seemed to be the artwork of the angels, in the form of frost, right there before our eyes. The message they wrote would never be the same as the message they had written the night before. This was made even more beautiful by the big-bulb Christmas lights Mom and Dad had strung around the perimeter of those frosted windows. The frost would cause the beautiful glow of the red, green, blue, and white lights to fan out all over the panes of glass. A seven-year-old boy could spend a glorious time in a very special world of light, which came only from the trimmed windows and a very warm fire burning in the fireplace. The freshly waxed, black asphalt tile on the living room floor would reflect all of those colors. The little living room became a room of wondrous warmth with colors that can only be seen again in your mind. When you became warm all over and with the smell the fire, it is so real forever.

The old circular throw rug was a place to lay and watch the dancing light on the ceiling. This was all before the tree was brought in and set up. It was something, how each year the lights just seemed to appear on the windows in late December. Who put them up there?

Dad came home from work one evening with a tree tied to the roof of his car. What an awesome sight—the king of my life with that giant tree on the roof of his 1946, black, Buick! In 1953, a miracle happened because someone gave Dad the tree. Dad stood on the running board of that old Buick. With the fluffy snowflakes falling on him, he untied the rope holding the tree. They seemed to be two inches in diameter. My four-year-old sister and I were jumping up and down with great joy. Then as he approached with this giant of a tree, we suddenly stopped. We both thought *how is he going to get that into our house?* He then yelled for us to get out of the way. Mom held the door wide open and somehow he squeezed that tree through that front door. We were mesmerized at the sight of that tree standing inside our little house. The scent of that pine would forever be an imprint on my mind as it wafted through the entire house. That smell is like a play button on a tape recorder. Every year it brings back memories of family. The mind is one of God's greatest gifts.

Boxes came out of the attic and other places not known to the children of this house. They were full of lights and decorations and Christmas. Dad attacked those lights. He would string those big bulbs on that giant, six-foot tall tree. Once in a while he would light up the house with his opinion of how the lights weren't working correctly or they were in the wrong place on the tree. Mom told us to stay back so we would not step on any light bulbs. Those strings of lights were all over that black tile floor, creating a constantly changing work of art. What a sight to behold. It was heaven, in that warm little house with Mom, Dad and my two sisters and later, my brother.

We would sit on the sofa with our feet up. When we finally got the OK to get down, we would go to the ornament boxes and pick one ornament to hold. Then it was time to wait patiently, while Mom decided where to strategically place every ornament on the tree. Sometimes Dad would tell us where a particular ornament had to be put in a very special place. The truth is every ornament was very important. When they all came together on that tree, with the angel on top, the joy in this little boy was so complete that I would cry. That very moment was so warm, full of holiday smells and the sounds of laughter. The colorful lights coming off the frosted glass added to the wonderful season. We were laughing in great joy because it just seemed that this time of year lasted for months. At least it was that way for us.

I could not wait to get home each school day to watch Santa Claus and Forgetful, his elf, on Channel

4, on our new television. It was only a half hour show, but Santa was counting down the days to Christmas. He always had some kind of emergency to overcome to keep on schedule. Santa was an overcomer and a leader.

My Aunt Aggie worked at a department store in Buffalo, and Mom would take us there to that glorious place called downtown. It was so magical to walk on that snow-covered sidewalk and look into those gigantic plate-glass windows. There would be displays of moving characters and new toys in action.

We had our own dream session surrounded by falling snow and the corner vendor as the smell of hot chocolate and cooking hotdogs hung in the air. The colored lights were everywhere you looked. We listened to the ringing of the Salvation Army bells while we looked into those windows. Those same sidewalks were busy with people doing their shopping and walking quickly about four feet behind us. It was like we had an agreement. They gave us room to look in the windows, and we did not get in their way as they were completing their missions.

After about an hour of looking at the many displays, the great moment came. We went into the great department store to see Santa. We had been prepared by our time at the windows. My sisters and I were ready for the time to place our order with the big man. Just walking through the store was a joy as you looked up to see smiling faces. There were colored lights and gold trees surrounded by flowing cotton, which was supposed to look like snow. Gigantic Christmas bulbs hung from the ceiling and they just dripped with the silvery, icicle decorations. Our ears could hear the Christmas songs throughout the store, as we approached the line to see Santa. Once you talked to him you got to go down a long slide right past the deer and snowman displays. Mom was their waiting with Dad, if he was not working.

Now that our mission was complete we headed for the car out in the snow-covered parking lot. We had a glorious ride home to our warm little home. The ride was made shorter by our conversation about what we had asked Santa for and on all the sights and sounds we had just experienced. My sisters and I were laughing and giggling with joy as we got out of Dad's car. We threw snowballs at each other as we walked to the front door of the house. Mom yelled, "Todge, stop throwing those snowballs at your sisters." They were laughing and squealing at the same time. It was such a joyous time to be alive. I know that God's angels had to be tickling us, because there was so much laughter. Wow!

Grandma's House

Going to the local Grandma's house was an adventure, which I looked forward to with great anticipation. I say that it was local because my other Grandma lived ninety miles away in the town of Palmyra, New York. In the fifties, ninety miles took about three hours to drive, but to a young boy it seemed like forever. Anyhow, Grandma would always have some special kind of dessert treat fixed for presentation, and I was so appreciative of it.

Grandma was from Poland, and although she could not talk English very well, she did manage to communicate with me. It was like there was a sixth sense, because she would say something in Polish and I would have a general idea of what she meant. Then I would answer her in English. As time went on, I would understand more and more of what she would say.

One day while eating a very special, baked cinnamon apple that Grandma had prepared, this seven year old realized that I just might be on the verge of learning the Polish language. This was quite a thought for a young boy to have.

Grandma and I spent a lot of time together on warm summer days in her garden and around her yard, as she would prune, plant, and talk to her green children. It seemed like she had a direct line to God, as she made and told the plants what to do. One day, I observed her talking to the plants and the trees and even scolding the birds for nibbling on some cherries. This was a very normal event. I actually thought that this is what all Grandmas did.

There was no alarm clock at her house to wake me in the morning, but there was something much better. Grandma would be in the kitchen before sunrise cooking and creating those magnificent scents, which would drift through the house like a river. I would be gently awakened by the scents of bacon and cinnamon bread. It made you wake up and follow the river upstream to its source. She never once woke me when she got out of that feather-filled bed that she slept in. It seemed to wrap right around you as you fell into it. She must have done that at the end of every day, because she was always doing something. Even when she was sitting, she would be peeling potatoes or apples or some other preparation. I don't remember her ever being sick. It was as if she was to be perpetual.

At the front of her house she had a sunroom that was full of plants that attested to Grandma's green thumb. She would have plants growing in the winter on that sun porch. The windows would be wet with the condensation on the panes of glass, but the room would be warm from the day's sun while winter lived outside. As the days grew shorter, they also grew colder and whiter. Inside Grandma's house, the smells of fresh baked coffee cake and apple pie would drift at one level. When you stood on your toes you could smell the fresh baked bread higher up. It was a sea of pleasure for the sense of smell. Sometimes the smells were so thick you could almost take a bite out of the air.

This was all leading to the festival we call Christmas. It was all I could do, just to keep from bursting with joy as all of my senses told me that the time of celebration was approaching. The anticipation and preparation for the actual day would take wonder- filled weeks. This time was also a festival on that sun porch. The condensation on the windows would turn to frost as the calendar was closing in on Christmas day. The multi-colored lights suddenly would appear on those many small panes of glass. Their many colors would shine through the plants on that sun porch at night with rainbows of light around the outside of the shadows. All this brilliant color on the frost-covered windows gave the room a complete and calming atmosphere, which could only be experienced at this time in this special and unique place. As the softly falling snow continued outside the window, it made me think that this is what it looked like when manna fell from the heavens. It made you feel like all was safe and you were taken care of. It was a comforting peace.

Stepping from the quietness of the sun porch through the door and into the festive dining room was like throwing open the canvas of a circus tent. There was joy in hearing the laughter and verbal banter of relatives who were just having a wonderful time together at the holiday. The room seemed to be brightly lit with the reflections off of the many shining faces. All of us grandchildren would think of games to play, and we would make up the rules and follow them or be banned from the games by the other participants. All of this play happened without adult supervision. The dining room table would seat ten people and always seemed to be the size of an aircraft carrier. It was only used at very special times of the year or when there was an honored guest of the family. Otherwise, we would eat at the kitchen table. This was where the younger grandchildren would eventually eat on those special occasions, because there was not enough room at the big table. The amount of food and the various kinds were always an adventure for the taste buds.

For me the highlight of the meal was the desserts, which were usually coated liberally with real whipped cream, a sugar icing, or a light coating of confectionary sugar. Some even had a coating of some type of cream cheese. The main courses were always the traditional ham and turkey with all the fixings. Everyone would bring their favorite dish to pass, and if you brought something different or new, there was great disappointment because we all looked forward to having those signature dishes. It was a family event of great magnitude, as far as I was concerned.

These festivities always seemed to occur at Thanksgiving, Easter, and of course Christmas. And what made Christmas unique was what happened before the grand dinner.

We would always enter Grandma's house through the kitchen entrance. We were hit in the face immediately by the great smells of everyone's dishes warming and the main courses cooking. This was a preview of the coming attractions on that dining room table. We would take off our boots and leave them by the stove. We would collect all the coats, and it was my job to take our coats to the front bedroom. You could stand in that bedroom doorway and look straight through the dining room right into the living room. You could see the most awesome sight a young boy could ever see. I should have reminded myself that Christmas is about Jesus, but I didn't.

The magnificent sight in front of me mesmerized me. I had to get closer in order to make sure that my eyes were not deceiving me. As I walked past the huge table on my left and the glass windows of the sunroom on my right, I came to the entrance of the living room. Looking to the wall straight across from the entrance were gifts on the floor piled up against the wall so high that my seven-year-old hand could not reach the top. It was a few years before I noticed that there was a couch under those gifts. The gifts were split up among ten grandchildren and ten adults. It didn't matter; it was still a remarkable display of God's grace and abundance on our family. It actually looked as if a giant slot had opened up in the ceiling above the couch. Then the presents just cascaded out of that slot, covering the couch and the floor.

The sight afterwards was almost as entertaining. We would make a pile of the wrapping paper and proceed to jump into it as if it were leaves in the fall. I would bury my sisters and cousins, and we would be giggling and become intoxicated in the sound and the moment of happiness. Then all the children would grab handfuls of the paper and take them to the old iron stove in the kitchen. This would consume the paper, and in the process heat the tea and coffee we were about to have, with the mountains of Christmas cookies. There was a huge amount because everyone would bring three batches of their best cookies to the celebration. The kitchen would always be very warm from the stove and the excitement generated heat from our bodies. The kitchen door would be propped open for a few minutes. We would get to see if the snow was going to make us stay later, while we were cooled like air-conditioning on a July day. You just didn't want any of it to end.

Grandma would just sit and watch all of our activities and giggle at the sight of her many grandchildren. Soon we all grew up and became teenagers, and the celebrations moved to our individual family homes. It was not the same for many years, until it was time to repeat the process with our own children. I am so grateful to have such a great model to follow for our celebration years.

When Grandma died it was a very different wake. I remember sitting around with the other grandchildren, remembering the fun and funny experiences we each had with Grandma. We just kept laughing as we related our stories to each other. It had to be very odd to see so much joy at a funeral. That is what Grandma left us all with.

That is our inheritance from her. Thank you, Grandma.

What a Difference a Bike Makes

The time had come for my very first bicycle. I knew this was the time, because Dad said it was. That made it true. The people next door to my Grandma's house were willing to sell a 20-inch bicycle for an extremely reasonable price, which Dad was able to buy. I did not know the brand name of the bike. It never entered my mind, anyhow. I can tell you that it was a gorgeous faded tan color with white stars, placed at random, on the front and back fenders. They were on the chain guard also. What really set this machine off were the two, tan leather saddlebags on the back fender. I was in heaven because it reminded me of Roy Rogers's horse, Trigger. He was a golden tan color, with saddlebags, and he was a star. Let's ride!

I had never ridden a two-wheeled bike before, so Dad did something that I never expected. He removed those beautiful saddlebags. They just made the bike harder to balance for a new rider. He looked at me and said, "Come on," as he wheeled the bike across the grass to a small hill behind Grandma's house. He backed that bike up to a small pine tree at the corner of that big white house. He said, "Get on." I managed to get on the seat myself and it felt so big. That's when Dad gave me his one piece of advice. He said, "Don't stop peddling," as he immediately gave me a very strong shove down the grassy hill and over the back yard.

It was a glorious ride, on a hot summer day, across a green carpet with the blue sky up above. It was so great to have the wind in my face and hair. It was great to move across the planet's surface faster than I could run. This was truly the greatest device for transportation of a young boy ever devised. Then it happened. The bike began to slow down because I was not peddling hard enough. I began to realize that it was going to tip over. I was preparing to dismount. The dismount would have been a two, if the Olympic committee graded it. The results were some grass stains and some brush burns. I made sure that the bike was all right. I ran with the bike back to the grassy hill where Dad was waiting. We did it all over again. By about the forth run, I had learned to turn the bike and use the brakes. I was on my way to expanding my world.

At the end of the day, Dad put the bike in the trunk of the car and brought it home. I was exhausted and exhilarated at the same time. The bruises just reminded me of each run. I went further and learned more on each of those launches made by Dad. Dad and Mom informed me that the bike was not to leave our yard until their permission was given. I did not even care because I knew that I had a lot to learn about this new steed before I tried to show off. I needed to work on my acquired, new skills. I just kept thinking, I have my very own first bicycle. Whoopee!

Sisterly Love

Time seems to drag so slowly when you are eleven years old. I think it is a good thing because then you have more time to try and correct the bad decisions you make. I loved waking up on the gorgeous sunny mornings of July. My sisters and I would have our pajamas on, as we would step from the back door of that tiny, cement block home. In our hands was a dish of watermelon for our breakfast. You had to pay attention to where you wanted to step. We were walking on the large rocks that Dad had placed inside a two-foot high cement wall. Eventually this would become an addition off the back of our home. This area was approximately ten-foot by ten-foot. It would be a few years before the cement would be poured over the large boulders which would act as reinforcements. Right now it was an area where you would walk carefully. It was the perfect spot to sit in the morning sun, eating watermelon and spitting the seeds at my squealing sisters, who would spit their seeds back at me. It was not a place to run around on. Mom would yell from inside the house for us to stop. We did when our watermelon was gone. It just seemed so great to be together in the sunshine, in our backyard, with the whole day of adventure ahead of each of us. I love my two sisters dearly.

The warmth of the July day would turn into very hot evenings. We would have all of the bedroom windows open to let in whatever breeze there was. We were usually in bed by nine thirty, as the sun slowly made its way below the horizon. It was time for the night games to begin. I would crawl out of my bed in the best imitation of a soldier that an eleven year old could muster, because I was on a mission. The consequence, if caught, could result in painful punishment. I would crawl on my belly out of my eight by ten- foot bedroom to my door. I would then make an immediate turn to my left, which was the entrance to my sisters' bedroom. It was extremely important to be slow and quiet. The floors, which were made of rough planking, had a tendency to creak. Fortunately, my body weight was not that of an adult, and I knew which boards to avoid. A bigger challenge was to keep my giggling inside myself. My sister Anne would tell my sister Becky to lie in her crib very quietly so as not to attract the boogey man. As I worked my way across the floor, Anne would tell Becky to move back against the wall and away from the raised bars of her crib. This prevented Becky from seeing me. Then she told Becky not to stick her feet out of the bars because the boogey man could bite off her toes. I could hear Becky's little three-year-old body hit the wall as she very quickly threw herself away from harms way. At the same time, I would be on the floor, rolling in silent laughter, under Becky's crib. I had all I could do to keep from laughing out loud. At the same time, I was excited about not being caught.

Anne would tell Becky not to move because boogey was now under her bed. At that instant, I would grab the springs, under the mattress of her crib, and then pull them down with a snap. Mom would yell from downstairs and tell us to stop. The excitement was almost too much to contain. Becky would squeal, and Anne would immediately tell her to be quiet or the boogey man could get real nasty. Becky would get real quiet. Now I would put my feet up against the springs and give her a bounce. Becky would scream out and then be very quiet. Mom would yell that if we did not go to sleep she was going to send Dad up. We all knew what that meant. Pain!

Becky eventually got fed up with this monster coming into their bedroom that summer. One night she just stuck her foot out through the bars of her crib. When she was not bitten, she slid over to the edge of her crib and got a look at the eleven-year-old boogey man under her bed. She looked me right in the eye and smiled. She screamed to Mom that there was a monster under her bed and she could not sleep. You know the rest of the story. She did have the last laugh. Anne just watched the whole thing from her box seat at this event. And that was the end of the boogey man.

Even though there was unspoken but healthy love between a brother and sister, there were still things that were off limits to my sisters, like our clubhouse in the woods. This was something very important to a boy who had turned thirteen. Anne wanted to get into that clubhouse in the worst way. To this day,

I do not understand why. One day she met me about half way to the clubhouse, in a little wooded area. I was walking home and she was walking towards the clubhouse. She demanded that I take her to the clubhouse and take her inside. When I answered her with a "no," she grabbed my cap pistol from my holster and ran to a large apple tree and climbed right up it. She climbed to a point where I knew the tree could not support two of us without the branches breaking. She held the cap pistol as a hostage and proceeded to yell down her demands. She held out for about ten minutes when, in her frustration, she threw the gun down at me. Anne was a very accurate thrower, because she hit the top of my head with the pistol. I fell to the ground, stunned by the impact to my head. As I moved to stand up on my feet, I felt a lump on top of my head. As I pulled my hand down I could feel wetness. There was blood on my hand. Not anything severe, but just the right amount to send Mom over the edge when she came looking for us. She asked what happened and I told her that Anne threw my gun down at me from high up in the tree. Anne was still up there. She knew she was going to get it. As her feet hit the ground, she was running for the house as fast as she could. Mom had come looking for us because she had been calling us for a while. When she did not get an answer she came looking for us with her weapon of choice. It was the dreaded black, hard rubber flyswatter. The hard rubber end was attached to a very thick wire handle. Mom could wheel back and with the perfect wrist action of a professional, flick the end of that fly swatter so it would come off with terrific velocity. Mom could hit a fly at twenty feet with this thing. We were easy targets.

Mom was angry with both of us when she first approached, so I just held out my hand. She saw the blood and I knew I was home free. Anne knew as she came down that tree that she had to be fast. Mom got her with a couple of swats to the behind. I was grinning as I took a slow jog toward our home about thirty feet ahead of Mom. Then I heard her yell, "You need to answer me when I call for you or tell me where you are going. You're not off the hook with me, smart guy." At that very instant the hard rubber end of the dreaded flyswatter caught me squarely and painfully in the behind. Mom explained that there would be more coming when we got in the house. I would always tell her where I was going after that. I also knew that if I made a wrong choice, there would be no working my way around the consequences. There were no time-outs in the game of life. We always looked out for each other when the chips were down. We knew that is the way Dad and Mom wanted it.

Time marched on and we all became a little older. One afternoon Mom was out grocery shopping. Anne, Becky and I were home alone. We would play games with each other, and this time it evolved into wrestling on the floor of the living room. This went on for quite a while. My sisters then realized that the two of them together could do a job on me. I decided I had to get the upper hand. I had to get out from under these two, who had managed to almost pin me to the floor. As I worked my way out from under them, I grabbed Becky's feet as I stood up. We had been wrestling in the center of a round rug, which was made up of braided pieces of cloth. These braids were then sewn together end to end and wound around to form concentric circles, which were all sewn together. As I stood up, with Becky's feet in my hands, I looked down at her while we were all laughing and giggling. I stepped back and off of the circular rug and was pulling Becky's feet toward me. She was face down and I wondered why she kept raising her head just an inch off the rug as I was pulling. At the same time I could barely hear her muffled yelling. Then I noticed that it was Becky yelling but her mouth was shut. About the same time I noticed that as I was pulling on her, the braided rug was moving right along with her. I dropped her feet and ran to her head to see tears rolling down her cheeks. As she lifted her head about an inch, I could see that her new braces had become tangled in the threads of the rug. She moved herself forward just a little and was released from their grip. Immediately she threw her head back and screamed. "You jerk, that really hurt." Then she jumped me and started punching me, but we all fell to the floor laughing at how she looked. Those threads hanging out of her mouth were a real sight. I stopped laughing just long enough to go get some scissors so we could trim her mouth. Anne made sure we got all the threads trimmed before Mom got home. As we were trimming we would just start giggling at the sight of all our fingers in Becky's tiny mouth. I know that episode did more to straighten her teeth than any doctor could do.

Mom got home and noticed the rug had moved. She looked right at Becky's red face and zoomed in for a look. We had missed one little piece of thread. How do Mom's do that? We had to tell her what had happened. Even Becky was laughing.

None of us ever wanted to hurt each other, but I can tell you that there were no more wrestling matches. We were all growing older and bigger. Most of all, we loved each other. Our lives were now developing beyond horseplay. Mom made sure we knew it.

Church Boy

Faith was becoming an important part of my life, but I did not even realize it was happening. Sunday mornings always seemed to be the sunniest. Mom would always call my name breaking the beautiful silence of sleeping in. She would stand by the side of the stairs and yell, at the top of her voice, at least it seemed that way, for me to get up. I knew that I would do as she had requested. All the while I was mumbling bad things about having to get up when the sheets had finally reached the perfect temperature. I proceeded to get dressed in my best clothes, go down stairs, and meet my sisters who were ready to leave for church. We could have gone out the front door, across the road, walked about two thousand feet through the field and been at the back door of the church. That would have been a great way to get there even if it would have been a little messy on our good clothes. Instead, Mom drove us around the block to the little church.

It was always much better after we got there, at least in my mind, because I did not want to go. My sisters did not mind it at all. We would get out of the car, walk up those front steps, and I would see my friends. Anne and Becky, my sisters, would see their friends too. We would then go our own ways as we entered the sanctuary. We very seldom sat together unless Mom was with us. It always seemed like there were two hundred people but maybe one hundred was a closer number. The short church service would end, and we would then go to our assigned class areas in the back of the church. As you went through the door to the right of the platform you entered a large room, which was divided, by the placement of chairs in various circles in the room. Each circle represented a different age group, so as you grew older, you would move to a different age group and a different circle of chairs. Each circle of chairs sat on its own piece of circular carpet. The goal was to get into the class in the balcony, which was where the teenagers had their class.

We used the Bible extensively for all lessons and were not given someone's interpretation of what it meant. We learned that it simply means what it says. This resulted in a very firm foundation for the rest of my life. I realized when I was around ten years old that Dad would go to Mass at seven in the morning before any of us were awake. He would faithfully go every Sunday. You see Dad was Catholic and Mom was a Baptist, so that is why we went to a Congregational church.

When our classes were all done, we would go back into the sanctuary for some more singing and then we were dismissed. As were walking out into the sunlight, we would be looking for the car. It would never show up. This was summertime in the 50's. We were safe to walk home, and Mom knew it. I would be grumbling on how she would make us go to church but she would not go. Then she would leave us and forget about us. I was just having my own pity party as I walked home with my sisters. They never seemed to want to join my party. They would just be looking at the trees and the flowers that were blooming. This would bring me out of my funk and back to the joy of the moment.

When we would arrive at our home and walk in that front door, the smell of bacon, eggs and toast would hit our nostrils like an avalanche. This would overwhelm all of our previous thoughts. The sight of the toast piled high on a plate with the jelly and honey running off of it and then down onto the plate was overwhelming. You could taste all of it long before you put it into your mouth. Sundays really were very special as we all came together for breakfast, and as with most special moments, you did not know it was special until many years later.

As the years passed, the time we spent walking home together turned out to be a great time for us to learn about each other. We would talk about school, our friends and what ever was happening in our lives at that time. The sight of my father cooking breakfast would always be a very comforting sight when we reached home again. We knew it was Sunday because Dad was laughing and cooking breakfast. The upper half of the front horse door was open and the Son filled our little home with so much joy. Mom would always remind us of that very fact. Dad would always respond by a simple nod of his head. All was right in our world.

The Dogs of My Youth

When you are twelve years old, a dog can have an effect on your life. Most of the time, it is a good effect. In my case it was two beagles that started a chain of events involving man's best friend. Their names were Lucky and Tippy. They spent most of their time in a dog pen made of chicken wire. The pen was about ten feet wide and twenty feet long. The doghouse was built right in the center of pen. The dogs would eat their food in the front yard of their house and make their deposits in the back yard of their house. It was a good, clean system. It was a beautiful July day and everyone was very excited about the Fourth of July celebration. We all had our fireworks and we were ready to set them off when we could.

One day I brought a firecracker with me to conduct an experiment in the dog pen. I entered the dog pen, and as always, I closed the gate behind me. When Lucky and Tippy heard the gate, they ran to greet me with wagging tails. I knelt down to pet the dogs. I noticed that the week's deposits behind the doghouse were all in a very neat pile. It was a large pile.

I did not smoke but Dad sure did, so it was very easy to get one of his cigarettes, break it in half and use it for an extension of the fuse on a firecracker.

This would give more time to escape the explosion. I slid the cigarette down onto the fuse. When it was lit it would give another five minutes of time, as the heat would eventually ignite the actual fuse, which would then burn very fast. I took the explosive, with the cigarette on the fuse and inserted it into a selected pile. It went in deeper than I thought so only the cigarette was showing. Lucky and Tippy were interested in this project, so they were sniffing and looking at my every move, very closely. The moment that I struck that match and lit that cigarette, sticking out of that pile, they both suddenly stood at attention. It was as if they had a vision of what was about to happen. That match started a whole chain of events along with the chemical reaction. The dogs stayed at attention for maybe two seconds. You could almost see their pupils dilate and the adrenalin start to flow in their bodies. They both exploded into action. Their legs were running, and the stones were flying in every direction. They were trying to get traction in the gravel, in the dog pen. When they did get traction, they seemed to move at the speed of light right past the doghouse. When making the turn to go into the house, stones from their flying paws were bouncing off of the house and hitting me. The two of them then were trying to get into the door of the doghouse, at the same time. Once they were in, they would not even stick a nose out. I was right behind them. I was now at the front of the doghouse so that the house was between the pile and me. The fuse was taking longer than I had anticipated. I was yelling to my friend, Bobby. These were his father's hunting dogs. Bobby finally came and opened the pen door and entered the pen.

As he closed the door he turned to look to see where I was. I knew the fuse must be lit. Already my imagination gave me visions of what could happen. It was all I could do to keep from laughing, as my mind had completed the event. Now real time had to catch up. I stuck my head out from the protection of the house to see where Bobby was and at that very instant the device went off. As intended! A hard piece of manure flew and hit me right between the eyes. This almost knocked me unconscious. The only thing, which kept me awake, was the screaming of Bobby. I managed to stand up and see a sight that very few will ever witness. Bobby was standing straight up with his arms sticking straight out from his sides. He had a coating of different shades of brown, covering him on the front and absolutely nothing but clean clothes on his backside. It was just like the sunlight hitting the moon. One side is covered with light and the other side is completely dark. The difference was the color of pink when Bobby opened his mouth to scream and the whiteness of his eyes when he opened them.

He walked very slowly and stiffly to the gate of the dog pen, as if he was a robot. That was when Bobby's mother came on the scene responding to his screaming. As her eyes scanned her son, she gasped and stuttered for him to stand still while she began to tell me what she thought of me. She was right and I knew it. She kept on yelling while she got a bucket of water and a sponge. I could have just walked away, but I knew she was a very kind person. And no matter how funny I thought this all was, she deserved my respect. I actually felt bad because of the labor I was putting her through. I also knew that when my Mom and Dad heard of this incident, there would be a punishment given out. This would result in being grounded along with a good old-fashion spanking.

I started to walk home after Bobby's mother told me to go home. I could not help but relive the event and have a good deep laugh. It was one of the few times in life when the actual event matched perfectly with the imagination. I did not have a motive to hurt anyone physically. When I reached my home I found that Bobby's mother had not even called my parents. In fact I don't think my parents even heard of this until I told them years later. Bobby never treated me as if he was mad at me. We remained friends. I guess everything came out in the wash.

Dogs would continue to be a factor into the following summer. I was thirteen that summer, and it seemed that they really were dog days filled with swimming, baseball, water balloons and a lot of bike riding. I loved to ride my bike everywhere. I polished, washed and maintained it because I bought it with my paper route money.

One day, Tom and I decided to take a good ride. Tom and I had become very good friends. In fact we are life-long friends to this day. Our time together was special even back then. We decided to wash our bikes. When we had finished, we wanted to take them for a spin to dry them off. We liked to watch them sparkle in the morning sun. We wanted to go down this road, which had a very steep hill on it. This would serve to blow the water off our bikes and cool us off at the same time. We crested the hill and started down.

We decided that this would be a great time to see what kind of top speed we could get out of these rigs. Just then, we both realized that two dogs were barking up a storm as they were coming after us. They had chosen the wrong angle to intercept us. With our increasing speed, they had to change their direction. At this point their path resembled an arc. These dogs were in trouble, and none of us knew it until one of them ran straight into a steel pipe holding a mailbox. The sound of his head hitting that pipe had a resounding pinging noise.

Tom and I looked at each other in total disbelief of what had just happened. We burst into uncontrollable laughter to the point that it was hard to control our bikes. Then an even more astounding thing happened. The second dog kept on his mission and wound up about two feet in front of both of our front tires. He was astounded also. You could see it in his confusion. What made it worse for him was that we were still accelerating. He would turn to the left and bark at my front wheel. Then he would turn to the right and bark at Tom's front wheel. At the same time we were gaining on him. He was running on total confusion because now the two front wheels of our bikes were right next to him. Our laughter suddenly turned to concern because we both knew what his next move was going to be. The wind was blowing in our ears. We had to yell at each other to communicate. I said, "He is going to turn into one of our front wheels. He was not going to stop. He has nowhere else to go." We continued our laughter and then it happened. That dog suddenly turned to the right and ran straight into the front wheel of Tom's bike. The impact caused the bike to turn to the right and forced Tom off the road and into a ditch. He was bouncing all over but managed to stay on the bike. I remember talking to myself and saying stay up on that bike, ride it baby.

Then I could see where he was heading. He made it up on the grass and out of the ditch. He was heading right for a fire hydrant and a telephone pole, which had a space between them of only three feet. Tom was still traveling at a very high rate of speed. If he put the brakes on, he would lose control and slide on the grass, right into those two very solid objects. I shouted, "Put it right in between them." Tom's eyes were clearly focused on the task at hand. His bike was bouncing all over, and yet, he put it right in between that pole and the hydrant. I knew in my heart that a guiding hand was upon him and that bike.

We slowed our bikes down, pulled them to the side of the road and laid them on the grass. We ran two or three steps and fell to the ground laughing together and reliving the entire episode. We were catching our breath and pausing in wonder that we were both safe and unhurt by all of this. We lay on that grass and looked up at the blue sky. We both said, almost in unison, what a wonderful day it was. We looked at each other, grinned and said, "Let's do it again." We got on our bikes and rode to the very top of the hill, turned and came blasting down it again. As we came to the spot where the dogs were, we were astounded to see those two dogs just sitting at the end of the driveway. They just watched as we rode by. It looked as if they were saying to each other, "We have learned our lesson but you two haven't, so we're going to watch you."

What really hit us as we were riding slowly home was that through all of this, those two dogs were not harmed and neither were we. The angels were all around us, protecting us. We learned you could not have the exact same experience twice. So learn to enjoy each day because that moment only comes around once.

The Principle of Ice Cream

*M*otivation is always a tremendous tool when used in a positive way. Mom knew how to motivate me. She wanted me to do the dishes after supper each night. This was not something very exciting to a twelve-year-old boy. Supper was an experience at our house. Mom would yell out that supper was ready. We would come to our small kitchen and sit down around our brand new red, oval kitchen table. It had chromed steel legs and matching red vinyl covered chromed steel chairs. I almost always sat at the end of the table with my back against the wall, with the side of the refrigerator to my left. It was so close that I could reach out my left hand and touch the fridge. My sisters were sitting to my left along the straight edge of the table, which was sticking straight out into the kitchen. Mom sat on the other end of the table in the middle of the kitchen with my Dad to my right. Mom was on the end because she was working the kitchen counter and the table. It was a very practical arrangement. For me it was a strategic arrangement.

The first time we had broccoli with our supper, this became very apparent. Dad was not always at supper because he worked two jobs. This gave Mom the opportunity to experiment with new foods or dishes to serve. Broccoli falls under the heading of new foods. We were not excited about this new food. Suddenly I had a brilliant idea in that light green kitchen with the red furniture. I could eat some of the broccoli and throw the rest behind the refrigerator. Thankfully, Mom would only give us a small serving of this new food. The first time that I made my move, I thought that my sister Anne's eyes were going to come out of her head, but she remained silent and acted as if nothing had happened. I was amazed at her silence until we had supper the next night. She ran to the table when supper was announced and sat in my seat under a very small protest from me. I suddenly realized her strategy. The new food for that night was fried burdocks from the field behind our house. I know because I am the one that Mom sent out to pick them. Anne knew it was her turn to use the magic refrigerator trick. The other part of the deal was the person sitting in the bonus seat had to sweep the floor after dinner. This was the only way that Mom would not find the evidence of our tactics. This was understood among all participants.

  Becky was far enough away from the seat that she never got a look at our activities. That cover was blown when Anne told Becky what was going on. They were going to sleep one night when the secret was told. I found out she knew when one evening she was sitting in the bonus seat after about six months of our covert actions. Spider, as my Dad called her because of her long legs, did not know about the clean up duties that went with the bonus seat. She almost blew our cover with Mom by not volunteering to sweep the floor after dinner. Anne jumped in and volunteered. She let Spider know that this could not happen again. It did not. Mom did not know for years about our pact and the special chair it involved. She just thought it was wonderful that we cleaned up after supper. We did not volunteer to clean when she was not experimenting on us. The code of silence was never broken until we had all graduated and had moved out of the house.

One night Dad was home for supper. We knew that when Dad was home we were not going to have any experimental foods to broaden our taste. We all made sure that we did not snack before supper because supper would be a good old-fashioned mashed potatoes and meat one. This would include a very common vegetable like corn or string beans. Mom announced that supper was ready and we all went and washed our hands. I made sure that I had a decent shirt on because Dad and Mom liked it to look like a decent place to eat. Dad gave the blessing, we began to pass the food and fill our plates with all of this real food. It smelled so good and we all knew that Mom was a good cook, especially when it came to the basic food groups. We must have looked like starved rats eating for the first time in weeks because Mom told us to slow down and save some room because tonight we have ice cream for dessert. I did what she said, and then I asked a dumb question in my excitement. I asked what flavor of ice cream it was. My Dad put down his fork and said, "You are not having any ice cream." I asked why and Dad said. "If you have to ask what flavor, you do not want it bad enough." I did not have ice cream that night. I thought that Dad was being mean.

A few days later Dad explained while he and I were riding in the car. He had seen starvation in India and that ice cream in most other counties of the world did not even exist. It was a luxury. The ice cream also represented his work for our family, and although he did not take it personally, my asking what flavor really did indicate that I was taking it for granted. Dad just wanted me to know what a privilege it is to live in this country. He told me that it is an everyday occurrence in our lives, but we need not take it for granted because it is not like this everywhere.

Dad's experience overseas made an imprint on his life. He did the same to us in so many ways but we did not realize it at the time.

Enjoy Where You Are!

Sitting in that classroom in late December, was a tremendous challenge to a twelve-year-old boy. We all kept looking out the huge school windows for those magnificent, white snowflakes. They had to come from the angel's hair that Mom was going to put on the tree when we got home from school. The school was always very warm and those huge, eight-foot tall windows were all steamed up. They were just waiting for our masterful marks to be put on them with our fingertips. The footprints across the windows were fun to make, but eventually you had to erase the easel so you could see outside and give the weather report to your friends. The report came with accuracy. It was wonderful to hear and actually witness. The snow was falling so heavily that it seemed to be blocking out the bright afternoon daylight. A boy certainly didn't think of the traffic problems the snow might be causing, except that there would not be much traffic by his house. Yes, the roads would be ours on this night out.

As we all headed for our school buses, we were so excited to see our breath. It was great to be alive in this downfall of white powder. On the way to the bus, we ducked a few snowballs and then lined up to get on the bus for the trip home. The ride was actually the time to set up appointments, meetings and assign groups for the afternoon and after dinner tournaments. I stepped off the bus and began the short walk to my house. I knew that once I got inside the door of that warm, cozy little house, the smell of the fireplace would just warm my very soul. Home was identified by all the senses. Two combinations told me, I was home. They were the fireplace burning and the smell of fresh baked bread.

Then Mom did it. She handed me the shovel. All she said was your father needs to get into the driveway. I knew I would be late for my appointments and meetings. That driveway was just gravel, so we didn't want to shovel it down to the dirt. The shovel was actually an old rusted coal shovel. Were we discouraged? We had people to meet and things to do. The first thing to do was to make sure we left a good hard snow pack and get this minor delay over with. Sometimes a friend might help, but no matter what, the job had to get done.

It was after dark that we seemed to be at our best in this white wonderland. We knew that the highway department was thinking of these kinds of evenings because they had strategically placed a telephone pole with a light on it by the end of our driveway. We thought this was for our night games. You just turn left leaving our driveway and you go right under our streetlight. As you continue down the street forty yards, you come to the top of the hill on our street. There was very little salt used on the roads at that time, so the side roads kept their icy white covering much longer. The snow falling gently under that streetlight was an invitation to fun.

This setting, along with your steel runner sled, and three or four friends meant it was time to run. We each carried our sleds with both hands, and in unison at the crest of that hill, our hill, we would all start running. On some inaudible signal we would belly flop on our sleds at the same time.

The goal was to see who could go the fastest and the farthest. This required keeping your sled on a straight path. You had to be very precise in your steering and smooth in all of your movements. The only sound you could hear was the sound of cold, hard, highly waxed and well-maintained steel runners, hissing, as they slipped across the ice covered road surface. It was that beautiful hissing sound, which became much louder if you had to make a correction in the course you were on. You could easily tell whom the most skillful drivers were, by listening to their steel runners talking in their own language of speed. I had inherited a good, soft touch from my father. At least, that's what I thought. So I knew I would win the majority of the time. A good night on the hill would result in fifteen to twenty good runs. The last three would almost always result in laughing and talking about why we were not fast on that night.

When the road was not completely ice covered we would resort to a game of full contact sledding. This involved the practice of swerving over towards your friend's sled and grabbing the side of his sled while he was trying to do the same thing to you. The victory was when you got a good hold of his sled and flipped him off it while avoiding the bare spots of pavement. The real champion learned how to hang on to the sled after flipping the opponent, and take his sled down the run with him. Your opponent would then have to walk to the end of the run to get his sled. Sometimes, two of us would be grabbing each other and concentrating so much on the goal, we would both wreck into the most glorious explosion of white, soft, powder entwined with our sleds and each other in the ditch. We would burst into laughter at the imagined sight of the wreck. We would replay the event with our own verbal videotape.

Building snow forts and hiding in the fifteen-foot-tall, evergreens that were along the road next to our streetlight was an excellent arrangement. We would wait for a person to walk under the street light and throw a snowball way up into the dark sky. The thrower couldn't even see the snowball once it went up above that street light The snowball would then make its arching decent down to earth where it hit its intended target. The whole event was very exciting to see because of the skill it took to estimate where the target would be. The intended targets were always unaware of what was coming down on them. The fact that three to five of us would launch at the same time meant that five snowballs were coming down out of the darkness ever so quietly. The target would have an astounded look on his face when he saw and heard that first snowball hit the ice-covered road. Instinct always told the target to run and then the other four or five snowballs would come smashing down on him and hopefully, hit him. After all that was the goal. This actually became a science project. One had to learn about speed, trajectory, timing, and most of all the judgment of where the target would be running. Teamwork was also needed in all the games we devised. If you broke our rules, you didn't participate. The laughter and friendship created an atmosphere, which could only lead to one outcome, success.

Wondrous thoughts of what we would do tomorrow and talk of what we had done yesterday caused many people to want to be a part of what we had. We didn't really know how wonderful it was on those gentle nights filled with snowflakes on our tongues. A slow walk home to the warmth and love of our little homes awaited us. The winter was never cold to us. Winter was hot and sweaty with the constant movement, laughter and friends having fun together.

Life in the Hallway

The flexibility of a child is truly an awesome thing and should be carried on into adulthood. I was about twelve years old when my Grandmother, my Mom's mother, came to stay during August one summer. This was a big change for me because Grandma would sleep in my room. We lived in a very small house of about seven hundred square feet. This was for four children and two adults. We just knew it as our home and really never thought of it as very small at the time.

We had a living room, a kitchen, Mom and Dad's bedroom and a bathroom on the first floor, with a hallway between the bedroom and bathroom. This hallway led to the narrow stairway and the two bedrooms upstairs. As you entered the hallway from the living room, an immediate right or left would put you in Dad's bedroom or the bathroom. If you continued down the hallway another eight feet you would hit the staircase, which led upstairs. The total width of the hallway was about six feet. There was also a desk against one wall in this hallway. When Grandma came we would set up a cot in the hallway and this would become my bedroom. It was just something that we did, and we all knew it was out of necessity.

This one particular year Grandma stayed past

Christmas. To this day I don't know if there was a special reason. In fact, I think she stayed until spring. It was very memorable for all the right reasons.

The hallway was a high traffic area and this meant that it was a great place to harass my two sisters as they went off to bed or to the bathroom. The downside was that they could return the favor after I went to sleep. This changed as time went on and the novelty of the situation wore off. Everyone had to go by me sooner or later since I was right next to the bathroom. Having only one bathroom in a house with seven people added to the business of this one area of the house. What made this time so memorable was Christmas of that year. Family in that little house became so important at that time of year.

I remember Christmas morning because my sisters awakened me as they came down the stairway whispering very loudly to wake up or be jumped on from the stairs. This was entirely possible because there was no railing on the stairway. I had to wait for my sisters to go into the living room anyhow, so this was not a big deal to be awakened by them. I threw the covers off and put on my slippers. We were all so excited to come out of that hallway and see the beautiful tree. I plugged in the lights and just hoped that one of those lights was not burned out. The whole string would be out if one of them was out. Mom would use angel hair and a few icicles on the tree. The lights would just glisten off of them. It was dawn outside so we plugged in the window lights also. We just wanted all the lights on, for this was such a special time together and we knew it. It was also time to light the fireplace to give the room some heat. The living room floor was made of black asphalt tile. This would absorb the heat from the fireplace and glisten with a reflection when it was freshly waxed. I worked at keeping it that way by washing and waxing it for Mom. The lights played a tune of glory across the frosted panes of glass and onto the angel hair which was spell binding to a child. Add to that the smell of the fireplace and the giggles of the family, and we thought we had just a pinch of heaven in our home.

It was the last small gift, which turned out to be extremely special that year. Anne, my sister, pulled this small package out from under the tree and said, "What is this? It is very heavy for its size." She then said that it was for me and brought it over to me. She laid it on my lap. I proceeded to open the gift and was very shocked to find a small transistor radio. These were very expensive in 1958. I was one of the first of my friends to have such a device. I think I carried that radio with me everywhere over that Christmas vacation, and ran its battery down in the first few days. I remember going to bed, holding it to my ear and quietly listening to it as I lay on that cot in the hallway Christmas night. I was feeling so fortunate and blessed as I was taken away to other places and listened to far away stations.

It certainly did not matter where my bed was as long as I was in my home. Living and sleeping in the hallway never harmed who I was or am or how much my parents and sisters loved me. It's a good thing there were no social workers around us then.

Any Ball Game Will Do

Baseball was the first sport to really capture my attention. During the long glorious summers it seemed like there was a game somewhere in town everyday. I decided to play with only certain individuals like Dave, Bob and Lenny. We would play with three people and the batter in Bob's backyard.

The rules were that there would be a pitcher, two outfielders and a batter. The field was of shale stone so we didn't do much sliding. The batter would have to run to first base and back home to score a run. When he had three outs, the batter would then rotate to the outfield while an outfielder would then pitch. The former pitcher would now become the batter. A complete rotation would be called an inning. After a designated amount of innings, we would figure each persons amount of runs and he would be the winner of that game.

There was a rose bush hedge along the edge of Bob's property and all of them were full of thorns. If you hit the ball over that hedge it was considered a home run. We usually played until someone had to go home. This meant that one game could take hours. The small area of the backyard allowed us to play with only four people where a regular ball diamond would just be too big of an area to cover. We would always have funny things occur, and thus we would need a rules interpretation. We were our own rules committee. We all learned the art of negotiation and how to work with others for a mutual benefit.

One such incident was a result of frustration but caused a lasting rule change to affect our little game forever. Dave had hit a nice fast line drive to his right of center field. Bob finally got the ball out from under the rose bushes. It was not over the bushes, so it was still in play. He then picked it up and threw it to me. I now had to make a decision. Out of frustration, I took the ball and threw it at Dave as he rounded first base, headed back to home plate. The softball hit him very solidly in the back. No one knows if it was the force of the throw or the shock of the incident, but Dave went down on the ground. I then declared that Dave was out because I had hit him with the ball. Dave was crying when he got up off the ground and declared that he was going to quit playing. This somehow supported our idea that he was out. Thus it became a good rule. That is until I came up to bat. Suddenly, I realized how foolish this new rule was, but it was the rule. This meant that every hit was for the home run fence or you were playing dodge baseball. At first, this was great fun, but it very quickly lost its appeal. We returned to the original rules we had laid down because every time you threw the ball at the runner and missed, he would score.

Baseball was our summer staple, but as we became a little older, baseball would share just a little time with football. Football had very simple rules in our neighborhood. Stop the guy carrying the football. The playing field was the front yard of Bob's house. This was because unlike the backyard, the front yard was all grass. Sometimes two-hand touch would be played, and if we were all feeling tough that day, we would play tackle.

The main hazard was that one end zone was the famous rose bush hedge and the other was a stone driveway. When anyone scored on the rose bush end he would pay a very thorny price. One particular incident stands out in my mind. I had broken away and was on my way to a very certain touchdown on the rose bush end of the field. I was actually running away from the herd of opposition when it hit me on the top of the head. I had just reached the rose bushes for the score when the stone hit. I could not believe that someone would do such a thing. I was in pain and instantly became extremely angry. I turned around and faced those other players to see who had done this. I immediately started running back toward them screaming in anger and ready to punch out every last one of these cowards. Bob and the boys had a dazed look on their faces and backed way off to stay clear of the roundhouse punches I was throwing. They thought they were witnessing their first mental case. Through all the anger I reached up to touch the top of my head for the blood that was surely there from that stone. As I pulled down my hand in front of my face I was shocked to see a dark purple, thick fluid all over my hand. In unison all of us looked up to the sky to see a gigantic flock of birds flying over our heads. Every one of my friends fell to the ground, immediately and began rolling around in great laughter. I began to laugh too and then I began to cringe in disgust at the thought of what was upon my head. This game was done for the day. Now I knew why real football players wear helmets.

The Kite and the Snake

*S*ummer is always a glorious time to be outside and dreaming of things to do and places to see. This summer was very warm with a fantastic breeze off of Lake Erie, which was about two miles from my home. For some reason I never realized how close this grand sight was until I was a teenager.

The cool of the morning always would lead to the heat of the day. This cycle would produce a soft breeze that would have a sweet smell to it that would last until early evening. This was the perfect time to fly a kite. The breeze was warm and the sky was a gorgeous sight with all the reds, pinks, blues and puffy white clouds. The grass would bend over ever so slightly in the breeze and actually look like waves in the ocean. You could see the beautiful pine trees dancing with one another in a back and forth motion. This often seemed like a stage show. The maples and willows seemed to hear an altogether different song and did an altogether different dance.

All of these sights and sounds sent a very exciting message that said go get the ball of string and tie it to the kite. It is time to go out and catch the elusive breeze that would now cause my kite to dance. I took the kite from Dad's garage and tied the end of string from the ball to the main center string on the kite. As

I walked out of the garage, I could hear, feel, and see the music of the wind begin to play on the kite. The dark blue, tissue-thin, paper would snap to tightness and pull on the string as the breeze caught it. The paper refused to tear. It was almost as if the kite was saying, "Let me go, now!" The paper would continue to snap and crack its orders in the breeze. I walked through Dad's garden to the small woods and onto the open field behind my home.

    This field had no trees but it did have some ditches and a couple of two-foot high anthills, which would be of concern when launch time came. I made a mental note of where all of these hazards were and plotted my course for the launching run. I stood very still to feel which way the wind was blowing. As I stood there, the breeze ruffled through my blonde hair and the fragrance of the field grass and the field flowers filled my nose with a glorious aroma. The scents never leave your brain. When you smell them again, you think of the warmth of summer, home, and a relaxed time of life. God lets you replay it over and over for your joy.

    The paper snapped and tugged at my hand as if to remind me of why we were here. The kite was telling me with each tug, "It's time, and it's time now." As we ran across the field the kite took flight in just three steps. It seemed to leap into the air with the skinny little string keeping it from its total freedom. There were thin white strips of torn bed sheet, as a tail, to stabilize the kite in the wind. What a sight to behold. The dark blue kite began to dance as if it was standing on a white leg, and the sight of all this against the light blues and pinks and reds of the evening sky could take your breath away. Looking up at that one hundred yards of curving string made you forget any cares you may have had that day.

As I continued to very slowly let out more string, I didn't remember the small bush I must have stepped into with my right leg. I kept my concentration on the kite, but I noticed that the pressure of the branches from the bush was increasing around my leg. That certainly did not make any sense. I stepped back to get out of the bush, but the pressure was now moving slowly up my leg. I decided to look down at my leg. Terror went through my entire body at what I saw. This was not the branch of a tree or bush. It had a white body with black blotches on it. To me it looked like the fabled, anaconda wrapped around my right leg in two coils. Suddenly there was only one thought. Get this thing off of me right now! The adrenalin must have been flowing so hard that it smelled. All I know is that I could have kicked an eighty-yard field goal, with the force of the kick that sent that two foot long snake flying off my leg and spinning through the air. The sprint back to my yard must have been at world record speed. As I stood in that back yard and calmed down, I knew that no one was going to understand what had just occurred, and then it hit me. I had forgotten about the warmth of the sun, the breeze and my kite. I walked back to the scene and saw the ball of string on the ground about twenty feet past the site of the incident. My senses were now on high alert to everything around me. I slowly picked up the ball of string and followed it to the grounded kite.

The paper kite snapped its paper in the breeze as I lifted it off the ground and I knew right then that there would be more kite flying in this field because we had beat the chicken snake. The kite spoke louder of the joys to come the smells of the field and the sights of the sunsets. When I got home and went in the house, I told Dad about the snake. He very calmly asked if I had kicked it off. Since I answered yes, he just gave his approving nod and our lives all continued on.

Monopoly by Storm

One glorious Christmas, we received a game of Monopoly. We would play it once in a while, but it just seemed too complicated to keep our interest. Then a big snowstorm hit our little town and our attitudes changed. The roads were not plowed or salted. Actually, they were rarely salted, so when the time came to learn to drive, it was on the snow and ice covered roads. We just learned to sled on them. We knew we were in heaven because we were not having school. We would be outside playing in the white fluff all day. We would make snow fortresses, which had many chambers or rooms, and then we would modify them just because we could. There was really no one who would attack our forts except for my sisters who had to inspect our work. We changed our forts, just so they would not become familiar with our layouts. This was very important to twelve year olds.

We were also required to shovel out the driveway which at the time would lead to a snow filled road. As long as the road remained unplowed we could take breaks from the driveway and have snowball fights. When that plow came through, it made us angry and happy at the same time. We knew the plow driver was happy because we could see him laughing when he passed by our pristine driveway. We would stand at the end of the driveway and throw the snow up into our just completed work. The laughing just added to it. Then we would look at the shiny surface that the plow revealed and got to work cleaning the plow's mess so we could go sledding. What a sight at night to see the moon glisten on that icy surface. The moonlight reflecting on the snow would just light up the road for our night games. Night or day the reaction was the same. The long shadows caused by the sunlight would produce rainbows in the snow and sometimes even revealed the different colors of the snow. Sometimes it was light blue and sometimes it was pink. Being outside was always a new adventure, but we were always grateful to return to our warm homes.

The fireplace was roaring with fresh wood and supper was done. The excitement was at a fever pitch because Dad and Mom were going to play Monopoly. Even as we were setting up the game we knew that this was a very special time. The entire family of Dad, Mom, Anne, Becky and I were gathered around the table for an evening of family fun.

The card table was set up right in front of the fireplace. The sight of that room was dazzling with the light from the fireplace reflecting off of the black tile floors and the heat being absorbed into those black floors keeping your feet so cozy. The game went on until well after midnight and it was a barnburner. We would each become heated with the emotion of the deals. We had discovered the pace of the game.

We could hear the wind howling outside and

we would all let out a cheer as the weather became worse. We took a bathroom break and Dad walked over to the front door and took a look outside. We all ran over to get a look and could just barely see the street light at the end of our driveway. We could see that the snow was really drifting across the unplowed road. It was a Thursday and school was already cancelled for the next day. We all thought that we would play all night, but Dad knew we would not last. Mom said to leave the game set up and we would pick up where we left off the next day. We had never played a game where it would last for days. This game was very exciting.

When we awoke the next day, Dad could not get out to go to work because the roads were drifted over. Dad never missed work. Suddenly, while we were listening to the radio, the siren at the volunteer fire hall started blowing. Dad, being a volunteer fireman, had to leave. Someone in a snowplow picked him up. We later found out that Route 20 had been shut down because a tractor-trailer had rolled over on that highway, which passed by our town. Many people were taking refuge from the storm at the fire hall. Mom was a member of the Ladies Auxiliary, so she got a phone call to go over to the fire hall. They needed people to make sandwiches for those stranded at the fire hall and for the firemen working the emergency calls. Someone picked up Mom in a snowplow. She said that I was in charge and that I was not to leave my sisters for anything. We could see the back of the fire hall from our house because it was across the field and on the other side of the block.

The game continued as we bought up Dad and Mom's properties in an auction style. We had great fun arguing about it but we worked it out. We were really developing our bargaining skills. Mom came home after serving lunch to the stranded people and gave us a description of what was going on. She stated how grateful the people were. I thought that I was grateful to be warm and fed as I went out to the woodpile for more food for the fireplace. We were wheeling and dealing in the game when Dad got back and told us about the trucks and cars that were stuck all over Route 20. He said a total of ten vehicles were stranded on the road. That was a lot for our area since there was not a lot of traffic under normal conditions.

Dad gave me a box, and when I opened it, I saw a pair of green rubber boots. The type of boot that was high cut with the laces at the top of the boot. I immediately put them on. Dad said that each of the firemen got a pair from the trucker whose rig had overturned. I guess he was grateful for their help. Those boots meant that the only wetness my feet would ever feel again was that of my own sweat. I could now stay outside for as long as I wanted instead of having to come in when my feet got cold. Dad said when you put those on; always put two pair of socks on so the pair closest to your skin absorbs the sweat from your feet. It's like he could read my mind. Now I could really work that snow. Right after I had that thought,

Dad said now I could shovel the driveway without coming in to warm up my feet. He got this big grin as he turned away and said, "Let's make a pizza."

We began to work the dough and then stopped to let it rise when Dad said, "Let's start a new game so your mother and I can play again." The current game was two days old. My sisters and I had a two second meeting and said yes because this would be the second time in two days that we were all playing together. Dad did not have to go to work at either of his two jobs so it was a "yippee" day. The next day was Saturday so we had another two days of tournament Monopoly. What great fun crying and laughing and learning about money.

The seasons always change and life goes on, but we were still into the game when the warm, spring rains came. This also meant that we would have thunderstorms and sometimes lose power. One night, at about five o'clock, a thunderstorm hit and it knocked out our power. We all looked at each other and without a word being said, our training went into effect. We all got great big grins, as we went to work. I went out to the woodpile and got wood for the fireplace while Anne and Becky were finding and lighting all the candles anyone would ever need. I was getting a great fire going when all of us noticed Dad standing at the front door with a camera in his hand. He was staring out the front door with a look of astonishment on his face. It was dusk and as we approached his back, we were all struck with silence and wonder at the glorious sight. The sun was setting behind our home and sending its golden rays of light in front of our home, turning the trees to an amber color. The lawn and the tall field grass in the field across the street were a golden color also. The sky was a gray, black color behind all this gold. Among all of this gold was our little, glowing, white church. The church was about three hundred yards straight across the field from us. Out of those dark clouds came the arch of a brilliant rainbow. As you followed the arch of colors that were so intense down to the ground, it was as if the arch was going right inside of the glowing, white church. It seemed that our collective breath was taken away at that very moment. It was as if we were being told out loud that God was protecting us. Dad lifted the camera and took a picture. He stood there silently for a few minutes more as the revealing sun went behind our home. He turned and said very softly more rain is coming and it may be a very thunderous night. We played Monopoly all that night and only noticed the storm in the background because we were not afraid. We rested and picked it up again the next day. That night the storm had left. As we ate supper, we bragged on how we had made our deals in the game as we enjoyed the warmth and protection of our cement block home and our family. God himself told us it was so!

The Black Box in My Room

The summer before I entered the eighth grade was a very melodic time in my life. My friend Doug had introduced me to music on the radio in 1955 but it just did not interest me at that time. Time marches on. Your life prepares you for your next steps if you let it. It just seemed that the music was now telling me a very important story. Actually I was ready to listen. I remember wondering how someone could get very excited about some song on the radio. Now, I had become one of those people.

At first, I was just caught up by a pretty melody or a very catchy tune. This made sense to me because Dad always said that intelligent people would listen to symphonic music. I knew that Dad was right. Mom would back him up, so I just figured that symphonic music was the only real music and that was the end of it. That, of course, changed when I started listening to the radio.

The sun was high in the sky on a July morning in 1959 and I decided to put the windows of Dad's 55 Ford station wagon down and enjoy the car radio, for just a few minutes. It was about eleven o'clock in the morning. The next thing I knew an hour had passed by. I was immediately enchanted by the announcers and fell in love with an instrumental recording called

"Because They're Young." It was a very natural thing to like this type of music first because I had been used to hearing symphonic music. I was so enchanted that I saved my money and went out and bought my very first 45 rpm record of that song. It was the only record I had. I played it over and over in my Dad's garage. He was not in the garage at the time, of course. I would spend much of my time listening to the radio and did not realize I was almost becoming addicted to this music. I think Mom and Dad knew I was infatuated with this thing. Mom decided to give me this old, 1947 radio. It was all black in color and about twelve inches long and twelve inches high and about six inches in depth. It had a very large dial for tuning in the stations. The dial was about four inches in diameter. The dial was black with small white numbers on it. It would whistle, howl, and hum when you first turned it on because it had tubes. These had to warm up for you to get the station to come in. It was almost like the radio was telling you to back off and let it warm up before you asked it to do any work. A small knob that was about one inch in diameter controlled the volume. I always made sure that the volume was turned down when I turned it off in my bedroom. If I had not done this, the radio would be screaming at everyone in the house the next time I turned it on. It was a very loud complainer if you did not treat it respectfully.

This black box of sound was left at my command. In my room, I utilized it extensively. As the sun would set, I would go to my desk in my room, turn on my light and then turn on my radio. I allowed the black box about ten minutes of warm up time and then ever so slightly and slowly, turned up the volume. Then it would be time to tune it to my favorite station, KB. Some of the songs would be very mellow or sad. Others would be so joyous; you could almost do cartwheels to them. As the temperature dropped outside, and the days grew shorter, I would spend more time in my room listening to songs and the stories they told. The disc jockeys would sometimes tell a story, in order to introduce a song. It seemed as if he was looking right into my life. I would hear a song and think of the girl I liked, at the time. If only I could just say those words to her like the song did. Another song would be how I felt about her. This was not the only thing I thought of because there were other things in my life. I just knew I was not spending as much of my time building snow forts anymore. I guess I was getting involved with life.

  The seasons changed. The snow would bring Christmas songs and all the joy I have always felt at that time of year. The songs just seemed to make your body warm and your heart tingle. One Saturday between Thanksgiving and Christmas, I was washing the black asphalt tile floor, in the living room, for my Mom. I was just getting ready to put some wax on the floor, and I was actually excited about this. I knew how glorious it would all look reflecting the fireplace and lights. There was love on every face that walked in that front horse door, as we called it. You could open the top half of the door and leave the bottom half closed. It was unique and gave visual security but still let the outdoors into the room. I had the top half of the horse door open as the first snow of the season was falling with those giant one-inch flakes against a back drop of clouds and sometimes blue sky. The sun would go in and out of the snow filled clouds and present rainbows of color across the black tile floor. Mom and my sisters were out, and Dad was working that morning. I had just finished applying the wax to the second half of the floor. I would do one half of the floor and after that would dry I would do the other half so you could still walk through the living room during the waxing procedure.

I was standing at the horse door watching the snowfall, and the song Jingle Bell Rock came on. I was enjoying that song so much that I started dancing. As I jumped and spun around, the joy of the season just kept building in my heart. I thought I would burst like a balloon. As the song came to an end I jumped up and slapped the wall above the arch leading to the kitchen. I felt a very sharp pain in my index finger as I pulled my hand down from that archway. I stood there and saw the source of the pain. A pin was sticking completely through my finger and out the other side. It just missed the bone on the way through. There was only one way to get it out so I grabbed it and pulled it all the way out the other side of my finger. I ran the finger under the cold, water faucet. I thought, what is a two inch long needle doing up there. The song Sleigh Ride interrupted that very thought. Nothing would stop me from enjoying the music and joyous feeling. The news came on, followed by the weather and the announcement that it would be a white Christmas. I never did find out what that needle was doing up there but that weather report was exactly what the doctor ordered.

    That evening I went to my room and turned on the black box. I went back downstairs as I waited for the black box to warm up. As I entered the living room the fireplace glowed in that freshly waxed floor and I could feel the warmth coming right off that black floor. The colored lights in the windows on each side of the fireplace and the large flakes falling outside caused me to think that if this is so warm and wonderful what must heaven be like? I slowly turned just soaking up the entire atmosphere and returned to my room.

    As I entered my room, I could see and hear a passenger train coming through on the tracks, which were about a half-mile across an open field from my house. Those people were going somewhere, and so was I, as I turned up the volume on the black box. The news was on and although it was mostly local, the national news would always take you on a journey. We never thought of the national news having an effect on our lives, but that started to change. The music would come back on. The words were starting to mean a lot and the black box would set a mood in my room. The words to the music were for someone special in my life. Who would that someone special be and what would she look like?

Oh! To Read

*I*t was the best of times and the best of time. We did not always realize that it was a great time to be alive. After all we were in eighth grade, the girls were looking pretty good, and I had a best friend in Tom. Life was becoming very exciting. Every great adventure was full of surprises. This was my own fault because sometimes I would do something goofy and not really know why. Sometimes it would work out good and sometimes it would not. I just stopped thinking that far ahead. It is like I would have a short circuit in my brain. I guess that what eighth grade is all about.

One day, we were taking a mid-term exam in history class, from Mrs. Bockmier. She was a tall, thin lady with thinning red hair. She always stood very straight and had an elegant way about her. It just seemed like the normal thing to do was to respect her. She was at the end of her career, but she clearly loved what she was doing. We loved her back. We just did not say those words.

My desk was moved right up against the blackboard in the front of the room. Mrs. Bockmier had assigned me that seat for some strange reason. If I turned my head to the left, Mrs. Bockmier's desk was about six feet away. The chalk tray was directly in front of me and in it sat a three-foot long eraser. It was as if this object had a voice because it kept getting my attention while I was taking my exam. In fact, as I wrote my answers with my right hand, I could caress that eraser with my left. Then I would answer its call by sliding it back and forth in the chalk tray ever so slightly and slowly. This action was meant to cause the eraser to pick up as much chalk dust as physically possible. I wanted it saturated with the white dust. My right hand had finished the task of the test but the left hand was working even harder at its task. I put my pen down and began to giggle to myself as my mind was already in the fast forward mode. I was imagining what was going to happen next. I could see it all as plain as day. The great part was that I could replay it over and over again in my mind. I started laughing even more. I was enjoying this so much that I wanted everyone else to share in my joy. So I made one of those eighth grade decisions based strictly on the flow of the juices of emotion. I knew I had to make this come to life so that all of my friends could enjoy this too.

Without even thinking of the consequences, I picked up that three-foot long, chalk soaked eraser. As I held it in my hand for only an instant, Mrs. Bockmier's words, in which she had leaned over and spoke to me one minute before, rang in my ears. She had said, "I am stepping out of the room for only two minutes, so behave, you are taking a test." I knew I had only one minute and I could see Tom sitting there right next to the door that Mrs. Bockmier had walked out of. The door was at the very back of the room. The temptation was just overwhelming. I let that three-foot long eraser fly. I had seen it wrap around Tom's head in a cloud of chalk dust. It fell to the floor leaving a white chalk ring around Tom's head. That is what caused me to giggle earlier. In real life, the eraser did hit him in the head with a magnificent explosion of white powder and a lot of coughing on Tom's part. However, it did not wrap around his head but just fell to the floor leaving a pile of dust on the floor. As the eraser bounced on the floor, twice, it seemed to stand on end for an instant just as Mrs. Bockmier walked in the door. It was standing at attention for her and then it just quietly fell over at her feet. She very quietly looked down at it. Then she bent down and carefully picked it up. Her eyes immediately went to the front of the room. I sat at the front of that room in disbelief on how this had all played out. I knew I was done and I would receive my just reward from Mom when I got home. Mrs. Bockmier came to the front of the room. She carefully placed the eraser in the chalk tray behind her desk. Her lips were tightly stretched across her face as she stared at me. She slowly approached me, leaned over and asked very softly, "Did you get out of your seat while I was gone?" I said "No." She knew I would not lie. She nodded and turned and sat down at her desk.

  I was astounded at my stupidity and Mrs. Bockmier's understanding. She proceeded to collect the test papers and continued her classroom procedures of having us slide our desks back into the neat rows. When we were done she called me to her desk at the end of the period. She asked if I read very much when I was at home or away from the school. I told her that I read comic books on the army or World War II books. She then asked me if I liked trains and I answered yes. She reached out to her bookshelf and pulled down a big two-inch thick book on the history of the railroads in America. I thanked her and took the heavy book home with me.

When I got home I began to look at the pictures and found them very interesting as I read the captions under the pictures. A few days later I decided to start reading the text of the book to find a deeper understanding of the pictures. I had been hooked by the wonder of the pictures and did not even realize it. I proceeded to devour the book over the next month, looking and then reading and then reading and looking. This was becoming great fun. I learned that Westinghouse invented air brakes. Then I found out that B.F. Goodrich lived thirty miles from my house, as did George Pullman. Pullman invented the sleeper railroad car. I was on a whole new adventure in this book and then it started to overflow into other books. This reading thing was very addictive.

Then one day I was in Mrs. Bockmier's class and an astounding thing happened. She asked the class who invented the air brake. There was silence in the room. I knew I was the only one who knew the answer and I did. What great fun it was to have everyone turn around with a look of "where did that come from" as I smugly sat there realizing that reading does have its rewards.

I suddenly felt that I was not stupid or slow. Nobody ever said those words to me; I just felt that everyone was much smarter. It was a revelation to find out they were not. I began to go to the library in the school just for fun. I would read a magazine or scan the history area for a book that sounded interesting to check out. I actually started to read the magazine articles instead of just looking at the pictures. I began to realize by reading and feeding my mind, I could imagine far more than any television program or picture book could show me. My mind was becoming the projection screen for whatever I would feed it through reading. Who could design such a device to do such a miracle? I could hit the replay button of my mind as often as I wanted to and enjoy it all over again.

I have been a reader ever since because Mrs. Bockmier entered my life and was the first teacher to truly hit the record button of my mind. She was placed there for a purpose, and I am grateful!

My Fishing Father

Fishing has become a great relaxation but it was not always that way. Dad loved to fish, and at first I could not understand why. Then he got me involved. Dad awakened me at five-thirty in the morning and away we went out the door. When the cold air hit me in the face, my brain said you are crazy to freeze and be up at this hour. My heart knew I was doing this to be with my Dad.

As father and son, we drove to the Niagara River and then subjected ourselves to a wet, cold day. We just wanted to play with sharp hooks, cold, wet fishing line, and dripping water all over us. Just touching the sides of the aluminum fishing boat would send a chill through your entire body. Then the tackle box would give this shriek scream as you moved it across the aluminum boat hull. It just seemed that your entire body was constantly being assaulted by these irritating sensations. Then when you caught a fish you would have all this cold, smelly, slime all over your hands from handling the fish. The only thing that would clean it off was the cold water from the Niagara River. How could anyone call this relaxing?

We would hook into a fish and none of these irritants mattered anymore. The thrill of that creature, fighting to get away, then pulling him in, not really knowing what kind of fish it was, turned out to be extremely exciting. This is exactly why Dad loved fishing so much. This was his relaxation.

His favorite fishing was for Musky or Northern Pike. Dad would take his eight-foot long rod and unreel about eight feet of line. He would then snap a steel leader, which was about three feet long, on the end of his braded line. This was all in preparation for the big lure that was to be attached. This lure was made of wood with two hinged joints. This would allow the lure to wiggle like a fish as it was pulled through the water. Dad would get the boat moving just a shade above idle and then drop the big lure over the side, into the water. The instant that the big jointed lure hit the water it began to have a swimming action like a real fish as it was being pulled through the water by the boat. Dad would then start letting the line out very slowly until the lure was about sixty to one hundred yards behind the boat. He would then take the rod and set it in this special rack or holding device. He would then concentrate on the tip of the rod to see if he had a fish on the line. Dad knew where all the weed beds were. He would steer the boat so that the lure would take a path right along the edge of those various weed beds, which was where the big Muskies lived.

When a big Musky would attack the lure, it would bend the rod and the vibration on the tip of the rod would stop. This was the signal for Dad to take the rod out of the rod holder and then give the rod a big jerk. This was done to make sure that at least one of the three treble hooks would be set into the fish's mouth somewhere. Dad said that sometimes the big, old, smart fish would take the lure and play with it like a cat plays with a mouse. In other words they were treating the lure like it was a real fish. So that is why Dad would give the strong jerk to the rod.

When Dad hooked into the first Musky, with me in the boat, it was exciting and shocking at the same time. As he reeled that fish up close to the boat, I was astounded at how big it was. It was about thirty-six inches in length. When it opened its mouth, I must have jumped back at the sight of all those teeth. I remember seeing the teeth of a barracuda in pictures and that is what this looked like to me. It was the nastiest mouth I had ever seen on a living creature. I grabbed the net and scooped that big fish up, tail first. I lifted him out of the water and into the boat. Everything was okay until I lowered that fish into the boat. It seemed to explode with movement the moment that its body touched the inside of that boat. The fish was flipping very violently and seemed to jump three feet straight up. As it did, the exposed hooks were flying around. Those teeth were looking sharper as that fish was snapping for its very life. In an instant, Dad stepped on that fish and preceded to wack it on the head with a baseball bat until he was sure it was dead. He then explained to me that this was the only way we would be safe in the boat, as he pointed to the fish's mouth. He did not wear gloves when he would handle a live one. This always astounded me because he had never been bitten or wounded by the teeth. I was not prepared for what I was to witness when we got home.

When we got home, Dad went to the back yard and laid newspaper across a wood table. He then lifted the fish out of a water soaked paper and threw it up on the table. He then took out a long, very sharp knife and cut open the fish's belly to see what the fish had been eating. I did not know at the time that he would always go through this same process with every fish he caught. I thought he was just being curious. He wanted to see what the fish had been eating so he could use the bait they wanted next time out. Some times the fish's belly would be full. They were not hitting the lure because they were hungry. He said that the lure just did something they did not like, or they might be protecting a nest so they hit the lure in anger. This generated much interest from my Mom and my sisters and really caused us to look forward to the cleaning of the fish. This was what it was called in order to get the meat which we enjoyed eating.

One morning Dad and I were fishing on the Georgian Bay in Canada. This was a magnificent place to do anything outdoors in the summer. We were fishing in a bay we called Deep Bay. You could look across the dark, blue water of the bay to the shoreline, where there was a stand of white birch trees. They looked as if they were standing at attention in the glacier, carved bay. Behind them were beautiful pine trees. The clear blue sky and the very bright sun of that morning, combined with the magnificent reflection of the pines and birches in the clear blue water, made you know you were in His picture. Even with all this beauty around, the fish were not biting on my lure.

A few seagulls were flying around, and in the boredom I said to my Dad that I could cast straight up and hook me a seagull. He laughed and said that will be the day. Dad did not know how much time I had spent in the backyard casting at various targets for distance and accuracy. I was prepared for the challenge. I picked out an incoming gull and took aim on where I figured the gull would be in his flight. With a snap of the wrist the tip of the rod bent under the tension of the casting movement and then the tip snapped forward as if to throw the lure out all by itself. The lure was released. Its mission was just like a missile in flight. The line followed the lure upward and glistened in the sun with the colors of the rainbow as the line chased after the bird.

Then, remarkably, the lure found its target and hit the gull right under the right wing. The gull was shocked and so was my Dad. It was instinct that told me to set the hook. The gull came down to the water and I reeled it in like any other catch. Dad was really laughing and so was I as the catch came closer to the boat. It came to the back of the boat as I reeled it in. That is where Dad always sat in the boat. He reached down to grab the gull, and it took hold of the back of Dad's hand. It did not release his flesh from its beak. Dad finally was able to unhook the bird with his other hand. The bird had to be pried loose from his hand. I was about ready to take a screwdriver and pry that bird's beak apart to get it off of my Dad's hand. When it finally let go and both of them were released from each other, that bird just sat on the surface of the water looking dumbfounded but virtually unharmed. As we drifted away from the bird we just laughed and laughed. What a great time together. Fishing was the only time when Dad was truly relaxed. He loved being outside, and he loved it even more when he could see that his children loved it too.

We went out again the next day and caught six Northern Pike, in one hour. They were very tasty at supper that night. Now I was the one that was hooked on fishing. The cold, slimy fish smell disappeared and the time with Dad, doing his favorite hobby, was what counted.

Track Is the Ticket

Running was a big part of any young boy's life because he is running from something or to something. In my case it was to something. In fact, I know now that God used it to steer me towards my assignment in life.

I played baseball with my friends from the age of eight through high school. At the time I knew I could out run my friends in a foot race. I just never equated that with speed. I could always run them down in a short race of say two hundred yards or so.

It is puzzling that none of the physical education teachers ever saw that speed except for one. I loved baseball, so it seemed very natural to go out for the baseball team as a freshman in high school. The coach thought I should play first base. I was disappointed as a sophomore. I just thought I should have played more. I think that is a very common thought in most good athletes. I did not complain or talk to the other players about any of this because that was not what you did on a team.

In the spring of my junior year I went out for the baseball team again. We were in the spring training sessions and one day our practice was cut short because of rain. I was walking to the team room when I noticed the track team doing some starts on the tennis courts. They practiced in the rain. After questioning what exactly they were doing, I learned they were sprinters. They were practicing coming out of the starting blocks. This one very tall and confident fellow came over to me with a swagger and said, "You want to try this?" I said, "Sure." He then proceeded to instruct me on how to get into these starting block things. He was very patient and kind to me. He continued to explain the starting procedure and sequence of words involved in the start of a race. I realized that this was far more complicated than I thought. I was very surprised at the amount of thinking that was involved. You had to be sharp at all times. Dennis, my instructor, then asked if I wanted to try a start. I answered, "This is really neat, let's try it." I watched everything that Dennis did to get into his blocks right next to me. I did the same. A fellow sprinter gave the commands of set and clapped his hands. We both took off for about 60 yards across the tennis courts. I had beat Dennis. A very strange silence fell over the tennis court as we walked back to the starting blocks. Dennis became very silent, and I thought I had done something very wrong. I broke the silence when I asked him if I could try it again. There was only a nod of his head in a yes manner. I thought that maybe he was very tired. We ran again and we had the same results.

As we were walking back the second time, the track coach had just arrived. He said, "Do you want to try it again?" So we did and it was a tie. The coach just walked up to me and said, "You need to switch to track." I thought that I had just had a great time, and my mind was made up as I was walking to the team room.

When I got inside, some of the guys on the baseball team had been watching all that transpired and informed me that some of the guys on the track team ran to get the track coach to watch me run against Dennis. They said, "You beat him! Do you know who Dennis is?"

I answered, "No."

They said that he was the best sprinter in western New York. I was completely shocked. I really was in disbelief myself and also in disbelief that I had experienced this. Then the coach came into the team room and asked me if I had decided to run track. I said, "I think so."

He answered, "Good, because you just beat the best around here, twice." Now I suddenly realized why about twenty guys were so quiet on the tennis courts that day. I experienced immediate success on the track as the season progressed. I started to believe I was a good athlete.

That summer, some members of the track team decided to form a summer track club to compete in summer Olympic development meets. These were track meets where you would actually compete against Olympians in training on a handicap basis. As you became better, your handicap would decrease. As an example you may start five yards ahead in a 100-yard race, and as your time got better your handicap was decreased. The goal was to start along side the Olympians and be in the race for a spot on the team.

It was very heavy stuff to think about having your shot. This also put me in line for the junior Olympics in our town and the county. I won the 100- yard dash for our town. I proceeded to the county meet where I would run against the best from the city of Buffalo. I won there also.

All of these experiences led to a relationship with an official who was observing my actions and performance as a person and athlete. I first came in contact with Mr. Ambrose at a high school track meet in the village of East Aurora. He took me aside and instructed me on how I was practicing my starts to his cadence illegally. He very calmly told me he had to disqualify me if I continued. I did not argue but chose to remain silent and responded to him with a "yes sir." A bit later he walked over and explained how I could practice the starts legally. I really appreciated his advice and thought how wonderful because he could be just like the others and not take the time from his duties. He just smiled and then walked away. I saw Mr. Ambrose again at the Olympic development meets that summer and at the Junior Olympic meets. He stated that he had been watching my name in the paper and my running was progressing nicely. I thanked him and was surprised and honored that he noticed. He then proceeded to do his job as always. The winners at the Junior Olympics received medals and trophies and during the winners ceremony. Mr. Ambrose was a presenter; he presented me with the gold medal for my event. He then informed me that they were short of trophies so I would not be getting one. I was disappointed but I knew that was just how it was. I just responded with an okay. Mr. Ambrose knew how to make disappointment disappear. About three weeks later, I was jogging down the street where I lived, and a car passed by me. I saw the brake lights come on as it was now in front of me. The vehicle proceeded to back up to where I was. I thought he is probably lost and wants directions. The car stopped next to me and in front of the pine trees, which offered such great protection and joy for our winter games. I looked into the car at the same time the driver turned to look at me. My spirit jumped because it was Mr. Ambrose. I am sure he could see my surprise when I said his name. He put his car in park and said, "Ted, is this the street you live on?"

I answered, "Yes sir!"

He responded with, "This is a beautiful place to grow up." He turned his head away from me, and when he turned back he said, "I have something that is yours." He lifted two beautiful gold plated trophies through his car window and presented them to me. They were the trophies for the Junior Olympic victories. He just stated that he knew they were important to a champion. I was astonished and thanked him. He never left the seat of his car, and I can still remember the warmth of his smile and the glint in his eyes because he seemed to be as thrilled as I was. He proceeded to put his car in gear and said, "Ted, keep running son because it will take you somewhere!" He started to leave just as I thanked him again. I just stood in the road as he drove away. I looked down at the trophies in my hands and thought. This man had to find out where I lived. Then he had to drive twenty-five miles, one way, to deliver these to an unknown sixteen-year-old boy. This was a very special kind of man in my life. It was like he was an angel sent to nudge and guide me in the right way. His words were very prophetic. I continued running in my senior year of high school and also was a sprinter in the summer Olympic Development meets.

There are decisions that change your life. Dad had heard that there were some openings in the tool and die apprentice program at the local Ford plant. I went down, applied and went through the process of testing and interviewing, and to my father's amazement and mine, I was accepted. This made Dad very happy.

I continued to participate in the track meets that summer, and it was at one of those meets that the head track coach of a Buffalo college approached me. He said that he had been to a number of meets and observed my performance. He proceeded to tell me that he would like me to run on the college team. This of course meant that I would have to be a student at the college. I was astounded at these opportunities and how they occurred. I just did not think I would be going to college because I was not that smart. This is what I thought and what my Dad thought. Mom always said, "You can be what ever you set your mind to." Now I had to make a choice and it was very clear that it was my choice. I will become a tool and die person or go to college. I chose college and running. Over the coming years, automation would take the place of people in the tool and die position.

I had to call the track coach and tell him my decision. When I called, he immediately set up an appointment in his office about two days later. It all seemed to move so fast, and it seemed to be in someone else's control. The day of our appointment came, and as I entered the coach's office, fear set in. I realized how big the school was and then I reminded myself that this was a very good man. Then he said, "We are glad to have you on board." He then presented me with my very first training work out. I got up out of the chair very excited about what had happened and what was next in my life. I turned and walked toward the door to leave. I thanked the coach again, opened the door and made a step out the door. Suddenly, I realized that I had to have a major. I turned to the coach as I stood in the door and said, "Coach! What am I going to take?"

His eyes scanned my body from head to toe and then back up to my head. He leaned back and said, "You look like an Industrial Arts/Technology teacher."

I said," That sounds good." He then gave me instructions on who to see and what building their office was in. My head was whirling, and I no longer had time to think of fear. I graduated from that college and was the first of the Malinowski family to do so. I eventually was offered a position as teacher and track coach.

Mr. Ambrose was right! Running would take

me somewhere. It's the small decisions that really have the greatest effects on our lives.

Life Changing Coach

*A*s a freshman in high school, I walked to the locker room on a sunlit, fall afternoon. At four in the afternoon, the angle of the sun gave a hazy effect to the locker room as the rays of sunlight came through the windows at a very low angle. This reflected the dust particles in the air as they hit the row of lockers on the right wall of the team room. Charley was sitting on the bench, in his practice uniform and full pads. I had great respect for Charley and I asked him how I could join the football team. He explained what he had done to join and whom I should talk to. The next thing I knew, I was in those sweaty, smelly, pads getting the snot knocked out of me from every angle. I had to learn more about the game itself, and at times it all seemed very overwhelming. I had never played organized football before. After about three weeks, I decided I did not need to do this that badly, but I did not tell anyone.

One evening after doing the dinner dishes, Mom and I were in the car on the way to the drug store. This was where model airplanes were sold. I told Mom that I was definitely not enjoying the football practice and I was thinking about quitting. She very calmly said that would change if I would just give it three more weeks. In her wisdom she was right. It did start to be fun even though I was still getting my head handed to me. Sometimes I had it coming.

I had a classmate in my algebra class who was about six foot tall and I was five foot eight. He sat on the other side of the room from me. One noticeable quality about him was his very red hair. I would wait until the teacher was about to enter the room and then yell out "Hey, Red Rodent." The second day I did it he figured out who was yelling at him as I grinned and looked back at his angry red face. He just silently mouthed, I will get you. I think I must have been doing this for the thrill of his hunt. After class he came blasting out of that room into the hallway. The chase was on. It was all very exciting because I knew I could out run him. This went on for a week and two days. I would scream Red Rodent in the hallway and his head would turn so fast I thought it would come off of his neck. He would see me and take off in pursuit while I would be laughing away at his efforts.

Then it happened. I was on the junior varsity team and the J.V. coach announced that we were scrimmaging the varsity that afternoon. This was a sometimes occurrence and not out of the ordinary. We lined up for the first play and the play went away from me so I was just standing there. Then suddenly it seemed as though the entire world had decided to hit me and knock me to the ground. I lay there, face up, with a monster breathing through his facemask and looking straight into my helmet. I was so stunned by this painful hit that it took a second to figure out what had happened. Then this beast just said "Red Rodent huh!"

I only weighed about one hundred and forty pounds. The coach had me at a right guard position. I was one stringy, scared boy most of the time, but I learned the game. I now knew that if I could survive the blind side hit of Red Rodent, I could take most any hit. Football would now become fun.

At the beginning of my sophomore season the assistant J.V. coach saw that I could catch the football. He told me I was now an end. As the season came to a close, I was running plays from the fullback position. That is the position I played throughout my junior year.

I watched the University of Buffalo football replays of games on TV. I had noticed a player named Maue was very good. He played running back and was an outstanding defensive back. This was quite an accomplishment because U.B. was the best team in the northeast at that time. I told Mom, after watching one of the U.B. game replays that I wanted to be a starting running back. She just said, "Be patient, your time is coming." It was always, be patient and it will come to you.

Later that summer, I received a letter from school stating that we had a new head coach. The wind of change was in motion because coach Maue signed the letter. I remember reading that letter over and over at least fifty times that week. It was like a rebirth for our team and myself. To top it off, a person I already greatly admired for his performance on the field was an inspiration just by his signature. What was he like as a person? We all would find out in a matter of three weeks. We were about to be transformed by his will power.

I admired Coach Maue from day one. His first talk at our first practice was about winning. He explained that we would only have about eight plays to the right and the same to the left side of the line. We all looked at each other as he continued to say that we would not need a playbook because we were going to practice those plays until we could walk in our sleep through them. This was going to be work. Coach Maue said that once we had these plays perfected, we would have the time of our life playing football. This was a very different concept from having a playbook with about eighty plays in it, and you were to memorize them all.

I remember someone saying could you win with only eight plays. This was the conversation in the locker room. I quietly thought to myself, I believe him. This is Coach Maue, a member of a Lambert Trophy college team. It is not easy to take a losing attitude and make it a winning attitude, but the process was under way.

Coach Maue was about five feet ten inches tall and his assistant coach was about five feet eight. Both men were in very good shape. They could terrorize us at will because we were starting to submit to their ways. When I say terrorize, I mean in a very positive way. We greatly admired both Coach Maue and Coach Backus, who was the line coach. They were both in their mid twenties but to us they were examples of real men. They both exuded honesty, integrity and very high morals, but they also loved the idea of full contact at full speed. Every lineman was bigger, physically, than Coach Backus and yet he could knock any of them on their butt and they all knew it. We all knew that these men knew about commitment. They showed us through their actions how committed they were. You never mess with a committed person unless you are more committed.

Neither coach ever talked down to us but always looked deep into our eyes. That was scary at first, but then you knew the coach just wanted your total attention because he was giving you his. We were approached as winners from the day we received Coach Maue's letter from the previous summer.

On some practices the frustration became apparent. Coach Maue would grab the facemask of your helmet and yell, "Look at me and listen!" He would give only three to five word instructions. He wanted us to focus on the task and the game itself. He would always repeat that once you could do that, you would have fun playing the game. He always gave you a punch on the shoulder pads after his verbal blasting. At first we thought he was mad, but soon we learned that he was very focused. Champions are always that way. He was the first thoroughbred champion, outside of Dad, who was put into my life.

It was the first week of September, and we were practicing a play called the 26. It was a sweep with the fullback carrying the ball to the outside of the end. The tailback's job was to run downfield ahead of the fullback and find someone to block. I was the tailback, and I missed the block. Coach Maue just shook his head and called me over to him. He looked at me, as he said he could not believe I would run all that way, do all that work, and not complete the last part of the play. I needed to find someone and hit him with a block. That thought process enlightened me right there on the spot. I remembered that twenty-second lecture because it applies to all that we do in life. You can do all kinds of work to get to a certain point and then not complete the very last task. No matter how minor the task was, you come up short. We ran the play again, and I completed my assignment. I thought it was a profound event back then, and I do to this very day.

We went to our first game and got beat by the eventual league champion East Aurora by a score of 31 to 13. We actually started to play Coach's game in the fourth quarter. I came out of the game with about six minutes remaining. I was standing a little bit behind Coach Maue for about two plays when he exploded with what happened on the field. He turned around and there I was. He stated he had, had enough of this crap and at the same time, in a flash, he was reaching out with his right hand. As he went to grab the front part of my shoulder pads, below my neck, he raked his fingernails down the front of my neck. When his fingers reached the shoulder pads, he gripped on very tightly and yanked me over to his face. He looked me straight in the eyes and yelled,

"I want you to go in there and run a 28 sweep and score a touchdown now!" He then threw me towards the huddle at the center of the field. When my feet hit the ground I continued to run to the huddle and told Billy, our quarterback, Coach wants a 28 sweep. That meant I carried the ball around the right end. I did what Coach had said and we scored our first touchdown. What came to my mind much later was that he had commanded it. We executed the play as he said and it happened. I believe at that point we started to realize that we could be winners. The last six minutes of that game were actually fun just as he said it would be. We won the next four games.

Coach Maue and Backus were starting to have fun too. One practice they both came out in full pads and played pass defense against the backs and the receivers. We started laughing until the first pattern was run. The receiver was smacked to the ground and the pass was intercepted. We all got real serious, fast. They would hit us and yell, "Get up." Sometimes they would take the ball right out of our hands. These guys were not only tough, they were good. Coach Backus just amazed us with his running and leaping for such a little man. When we were done with practice, they were laughing at us and with us. We knew we had real men coaching us who loved us without saying so. Those two wanted to win in all that they did.

After practice, we were all talking when we were in the shower. We were comparing how they would blast us to the ground with a clean hit and then yell, "Get up and beat me next time." When you did beat them they would slap you on the helmet and yell, "Good job, that's how to do it, now do it on game day." We always hoped they would do it again, but they did not need to.

After every Saturday game, we had a dance in the evening. We never had any night games because lights cost too much. At one dance, both of our football coaches were the chaperones. For some of us on the team, this was really extra special. Then we found out that Coach Maue was bringing a date with him. She was a very attractive blond lady. Coach was very busy chaperoning when he walked over to me and asked me to dance with his date. He wanted me to take care of her because he was very busy and she was just standing around. He told me to treat her like a lady and proceeded to walk away. He must have noticed how nervous I had become because he stopped in his tracks, turned around, looked me in the eye and said, "Ted, just be the person that you are." I was so honored by his words and by his trust. That trust brings tears to my eyes as I am writing this. He has influenced my life in so many ways. I must say that he is a true hero in my life. He is a very humble man with an enormous heart. His trust and his life building sayings have profoundly affected my life. I think of him often and am very grateful that he was placed in my life by providence.

Coach made a statement about our team about 25 years later when I saw him. He said that some teams he had coached, had far more talent than our team but our team had an awesome desire to win, more than any other team he had coached. That is enough for me.

All of this because Mom said to stick it out for three more weeks and your time is coming.

Finding "The One"

The basketball games on Friday night were always fun to go to. If the team won, they were even more fun. Tom, Dave, Ron and I would always sit together and yell and talk and have a good time being friends. The game would be over at about 8:30 in the evening and for fifty cents one could go to the dance in the auxiliary gym. These dances were stand against the wall and watch affairs. Once in a while one of us would actually get enough nerve to ask a girl to dance. I don't think any of us realized that all those girls were just waiting for anyone of us to ask them to dance. It was better that none of the guys knew that. To us, it was almost like making a commitment just dancing with a girl. Of course, that was not how any of the girls saw it.

One Friday I purchased a six-inch in diameter sucker and proceeded to the water fountain where I soaked it with water a number of times until it became very sticky. As I entered the dance, I saw my friend Lance had already asked someone to dance. I very calmly walked over to Lance and slapped him on the cheek with that very sticky sucker. I thought for sure, that when Lance put his cheek against his partners, they would stick together. This was not a pleasant experience for him and he let me know it. This dance stuff was now becoming a very serious ritual to some of the participants. I did not know that my time was coming for such an experience.

My time came in my senior year. It was a March of Dimes dance. This one was seventy-five cents because it was for an important cause. I saw her there, and I slowly walked towards her. As I stood at attention in front of her, I asked her to dance, and she very softly said yes. Our first dance was a fast dance so we were apart, and I noticed her beautiful, long flowing, brown, hair. I was taken by the vision of God's very own creation. She smiled, and I was crazed in what seemed to be the most perfect smile I had ever seen. This different feeling was upon me, and I was completely infatuated in this vision. Nothing else existed but what I saw in front of me. She was wearing a pink, fluffy woven sweater with a v-neck. She had a gold heart shaped necklace on her neck. Her pleated skirt had a plaid pattern of blues and grays with a pink thread going through the plaid pattern. Her shoes were black flats with webbing over her toes, and she had gorgeous legs. She had my attention.

The next dance was a slow dance, and I asked her again. My heart jumped with her positive answer. Then it was announced that this was the last dance of the night. I had a feeling deep in my heart that this girl would be very special for the rest of my life. This feeling was shouting to me. I wondered what feeling she had. As we parted, I knew our lives were just starting to flow together. I watched from a distance as she walked off the dance floor and as she walked out into the cold night wind. I saw her beautiful, brown hair move around her shoulders as she disappeared into her father's car. I knew we were destined to be together, but did she?

It is really unique that when our emotions for someone increase, every song seems to be for you and your situation. It was as if The Beach Boys, The Lettermen and a new group called The Beatles were watching our lives and singing just for our hearts. I was astounded to find out that the girl I had danced with lived a half mile from my home.

The following Monday I saw her at school, and I had to ask her to the next dance. She accepted. Wow!

Every time I saw her, my whole being seemed to jump with a kind of calm excitement. The mystery is how and why this kind of thing happens. I did not ask that question then because I was lovesick on whatever the body produces to give you that wonderful feeling. It always starts so small and simple. I would look for her in the main school hallway as I walked with the guys on our normal morning patrol before homeroom. There she was! Focus is a very powerful thing. It was focus that caused me to completely ignore my patrol buddies and walk towards her. Nothing else existed at that very moment but the vision of her. There were many sounds at the student lockers. The morning talks about every event or the books falling from a locker shelf with a very loud whack did not distract me. It was like a gun going off, but I never heard it.

What I could hear was the soft swishing sound of her skirt. It was like the warm summer breezes gently swishing the tall field grass back and forth. I know I could hear her hair moving with that same sound, just a little softer as she walked. When she smiled as I approached, I could hear her lips move across her teeth and the very quiet opening and closing of those big brown eyes. All she said was hi! That's all it took to make the entire day. Oh! It was wonderful to be in high school. This whole experience became a daily habit that I did not want to kick.

My buddies just shook their heads because they were very quickly being replaced. Eventually each one of them would find his own experience. Only one of my buddies really had the same experience with his girl that I had. He just said, wow! I looked at him and he knew that I knew exactly what he meant.

In the cold days of that winter, we would take walks from our own homes and meet at the corner in between them and then walk together. We always would meet under the same streetlight. Sometimes the snow would be falling ever so slowly and gently. As I approached her, I could see her waiting in that light. Darkness was everywhere but where she was standing. The perfect white snow falling out of the heavens into the dark and then into the bright white light that encircled her. It was as if she was standing in a ball covered with glass. She put out her glove covered hand and just said hi! I took her hand and said hi as we walked out of the light and into the darkness together. The snow seemed to be like angel dust, protecting both of us. Suddenly, it was not cold, but we could see our breath. I do not think a car passed as we walked the snow-covered road to the overhead bridge. As we walked, we passed by a stand of pine trees, which were about twenty feet tall. The stand had to stretch for a good forth of a mile. Their branches sagging with the weight of the pure white snow was peaceful. A very slight gust of wind came up and swirled some of the fine powder up off of the pines as we walked by. Gently as a loving hand, the wind moved her hair next to and across my face. It seemed to wave her perfume to me. The air was so fresh and chilled that the scent seemed to be even stronger than normal. The warmth inside me caused the chill to leave. We just stopped walking and wrapped our arms around one another. The warmth of caring for each other is the great heater of life. There was no passionate attacking of each other but rather a very gentle embrace in the middle of what seemed like falling crystals. Any other type of embrace would have caused the crystal flakes to shatter and the pine tree branches to break. They were the only witnesses to a developing deep love.

There has never been another.

The Gifts from Others

*D*ad worked for a distribution company, which was owned by a family, who were very generous to my father. Dad could have worked for a car manufacturer but turned it down out of loyalty. Although he worked very long hours, sometimes he would bring home very unexpected surprises. One Friday in January, he brought home a six-wheeled vehicle, which could carry two people and some cargo behind the bench seat. The body was a dark red color with three big fat, balloon- type tires on each side. It certainly looked very strange sitting on that trailer behind Dad's station wagon. It was 1966 and these kinds of toys were extremely expensive and very rare. I couldn't imagine what a person would do with such a contraption. Dad knew exactly what we would be doing for the next month with this remarkable toy. We were far from monetary wealth, but we knew those who had wealth and were very generous with it.

Dad got into the machine and he looked like he was going to burst into a long, loud, yahoo! That is not how he was. Dad just smiled and gave an extremely approving nod of his head. The red color of the machine, against the beautiful white, clean and crunchy snow was really an awesome sight.

The big one inch flakes of snow, were beginning to fall and every once in a while the sun would burst forth, giving the effect of an old time photo flash going off. This would cause rainbows to flash on those big snowflakes. It did nothing to their taste as they struck our tongues.

Dad broke the silence of the moment when he said, "Get in." He turned the key to the left on that red dashboard, where a red light showed you the machine was on. The only other feature was a speedometer. There was one, small, straight, black, plastic seat with a formed backrest that was cold and hard but would soon be known as a back saver. The two-cycle engine burst into life and the smell of the oil and gasoline mixture was like perfume to a young boy's nostrils. The only thought was, what a toy this is. Dad pulled back on the two sticks, which controlled each side of the machine, separately. By pulling back on both sticks, both sides backed up with the same amount of power. Dad, ever so slowly, backed the machine off of the trailer and drove it on the flat, snow covered ground. He immediately took me on a trip to the summer fair with the ride that followed, Wow!

The rest of the month was a race to get home, fire up that beast and roar out of the yard in a plume of blue smoke with flying, powdered snow on the six-wheeled adventure. You just didn't know what was in store when you were blasting through the empty fields. In the early evening, my brother John and I were blasting through a field. We were sitting still when a dog came out after us. I started the machine and took off. The dog began to fall behind us but was persistently running after our white cloud of snow. I pulled back on one stick and pushed the other one full forward. The result was a perfect one hundred eighty degree turn at wide-open throttle. We were turning and sliding on the snow in one direction and when the machine came around to where it was pointing in the opposite direction, I pushed both sticks completely forward. We were now sliding backward until the tires got traction on the snow. The dog stopped running and in fact put his front paws out in front of him to stop. He seemed to come to attention and stare in disbelief because we were now chasing him faster and faster. It was as if he did a double take because it was something he had never seen before. The dog took off running. We were about fifteen yards behind him. As he was running, he kept turning to see if we were still coming. The dog turned and we turned with the same abruptness. He then headed for a ditch, which was about four feet deep, with some water in it. He jumped the stream and then stopped and turned. I stopped the machine at the edge of the ditch. It was now dusk so I turned on the headlights. The lights shinned on the dog's feet as he stood on a berm about four feet high on the other side of the ditch. I jammed both sticks forward and hit the gas. The machine lurched forward and went through the ditch and began to climb the berm. The headlights were now pointing up on the dog. It was as if he had a facial expression of utter amazement on his face. He finally regained his senses and took off into the safety of the darkness. This all took place in about four minutes. It seemed like half an hour of fun. I stopped the machine. My Brother and I laughed at this creature, which to us took on human qualities. We never had an experience with a dog and the machine again. They all seemed to stay clear of it.

My Sister Becky decided to try her hand at the machine. She was so excited to get her solo shot at driving the red monster. She left on her own and headed for the field that was behind our house. An hour later she walked into the house crying. She had managed to get three flat tires. We went out to the field to see the red machine sitting on top of an old bedspring someone had used to drag the soil for planting maybe ten years before. We all laughed because out of forty acres of field, she had to find the bedsprings. She was determined to drive the monster. After the tires were fixed, she took it out again but was rather timid with the machine so as not to break it.

We had many joyful rides that winter all because someone else had great bounty and grace and they were willing to share it with us. We were all very grateful.

Dad Under Fire

Dad made sure that I was always learning the importance of work and that money just did not grow on trees. He said that when I was sixteen, we would work together. True to his word, in the summer of my sixteenth year, we began by washing the beer trucks used by the distribution company he worked for.

Every Saturday morning, except for football season, we would go to a small restaurant and have a hard roll and a cup of coffee for breakfast. We then would read the sports section of the newspaper. It really was a very important time with Dad, sitting at the counter of various coffee shops, discussing what the pro-football teams would be doing or some other topic. That was a real rarity with Dad. He would ask if I was ready to go, and we would leave for the "shop" as he called it.

Once we got there we would each grab a bucket with wheels on it and a brush, along with a hand full of soap powder, which we threw into the bucket before we filled it with water. We each had a hose to soak down each truck before we washed it with the soapy brush. Then we would reach to the top of those trucks rinsing off the soap. There were about thirty trucks, and about twenty of them were inside. The few that were outside could be washed outside in the summer and rotated inside in the winter. Dad had it down to a system, and it worked very well.

One Saturday in late June, we were on our way to wash trucks at about 7:30 in the morning. Dad decided to stop at a restaurant in a local plaza about eight miles from our house. On the way Dad would have a cigarette. He would always crack his window because he knew I did not smoke. As he turned into the plaza parking lot, he just said, "We are going to this restaurant because they have better coffee." As we drove through the lot, the radio newsman was talking about a drive-by shooting in the city. The windows of some bar had been shot out.

Dad parked the car in the parking space and the radio went off when Dad turned the car off. We got out of the car and stepped into the brilliant sunlight on that, beautiful morning. As we walked to the curb in front of the restaurant, you could see the dark blue water of Lake Erie in the distance, along with Canada and the city of Buffalo skyline. It was as if you could jump from cloud to white puffy cloud right onto the white and gold colored buildings of the city about eight miles across the water. We were on the side of a hill looking down and over the Lake. It was a gorgeous sight and a very joyful morning to be alive and having time with Dad. We entered the restaurant through a glass door after walking past a twenty-foot long plate glass window, which was about six feet high, across the entire front of the restaurant.

As we walked over to the counter, you could see that it was shaped like the letter M with the indentation in the middle. Dad decided to pick the two seats that were in the center of the indentation so that the counter was curving around beside us on both sides of our seats. We were the only customers in this empty restaurant. As we leaned against the counter in front of us, the waiter came over and poured our coffee. He asked if we wanted any food. We both ordered a fried hard roll. The waiter walked back and gave our order to the cook.

Suddenly there was a very loud bang. My mind, in a split second, said that it was a gunshot. In the time it took my head to snap from looking at the waiter to looking to the front of the restaurant, Dad had already hit the deck and had his hand on my shoulder pulling me out of that seat as he shouted, "Get down." We were both on the floor, surrounded by the counter up above, when Dad yelled to cover my head. As we lay on the floor, for no more than two seconds, we heard two more very loud bangs. I knew that this had to be the same shooters from the city. After the second bang, the front plate glass window shattered and all the glass fragments were blown into the restaurant. The shards of glass blew right over the tops of the counters on each side of us on their way to the back of the room where you could hear the glass hitting the back wall of the restaurant. There was a combination of the tinkling of glass and the whoosh of the wind but not a single piece of anything ever struck either one of us. In the next instant Dad grabbed me by the back of my shirt and pulled me up off the floor. He said, "Let's get out of here now!" He was actually pushing me in the back as we moved faster and faster for the door. The only thing left was the aluminum framework that was supporting the glass. I became very concerned because the guys with the guns could still be out there in their car, but I never verbalized that thought because Dad knew what he was doing.

As we stepped off the curb in front of the restaurant and onto the pavement of the parking lot I turned to see the restaurant engulfed in flames. We began to run as the flames came out the front like a blowtorch. When we reached the car, Dad said get in and we drove further away from the flames. We both got out of the car and were standing with two of the workers from the restaurant. It was no more than four minutes since Dad had pulled me to the floor. Dad looked around quickly and asked, "Which one of you is the cook?" One of the workers said, "Neither one of us." Dad then muttered that he was still in there.

He then took about three quick steps toward the inferno, and I yelled, "No, you are not going in there!" as I grabbed the back of his shirt. A car broke through the smoke and was coming toward us. It was the cook who had gone out the back of the restaurant to save his car. I was so relieved because I didn't know how I would have held my Dad back from going in for that cook. We never did get our coffee and hard roll. We got into the car after the police took our names and went to another restaurant for our hard roll and coffee. That's when Dad explained what actually had happened.

There was a paint store next to the restaurant

and some old paint cans mixed with some oily rags caught fire by spontaneous combustion. The very loud bangs were the first of many paint cans that blew up. These explosions blew out the front of the paint store window. When this happened, the air in the store blew out the front also. This resulted in the air in the restaurant, where we were, being sucked out and over to the paint store. That was why the plate glass window was pulled into the restaurant in a thousand pieces. It caused a partial vacuum in the restaurant. The paint store had all the fuel it needed to be a raging inferno, which only caused more oil based paint cans to blow and add more fuel causing the blowtorch effect.

There were no gunmen. My imagination had just run rampant. What Dad did that day was as if he was on automatic pilot. I witnessed him in action in a critical situation, and he made all the right decisions without hesitation. I am sure that his military experience and training, along with a great heart to help, had a giant input on all of this. I gained a great respect for the man he was and even more admiration. I felt very blessed that he was my Dad. He said nothing about what happened to anyone, unless they asked. His answer contained no description or detail. It was no brag, just facts. I heard him describe it as an interesting morning. He was the model for the phrase, actions speak louder than words.

As I think back to some of the things he did, I am listening to him more intently now than when he was on this earth with me. I know who his teacher is.

Contact T.S. Malinowski
or order more copies of this book at

TATE PUBLISHING, LLC

127 East Trade Center Terrace
Mustang, Oklahoma 73064

(888) 361 - 9473

Tate Publishing, LLC

www.tatepublishing.com